LIFE IN COMM(

LIFE IN COMMON

AN ESSAY IN GENERAL ANTHROPOLOGY

by TZVETAN TODOROV

Translated by Katherine Golsan and Lucy Golsan

With a new afterword by the author

University of Nebraska Press

Lincoln and London

Originally published as
La Vie commune: Essai d'anthropologie générale
© Editions du Seuil, 1995
Translation and afterword © 2001
by the University of Nebraska Press
All rights reserved
Manufactured in the United States of America
♾
Library of Congress Cataloging-in-Publication Data
Todorov, Tzvetan, 1939–
[Vie commune. English]
Life in common : an essay in general anthropology / by Tzvetan Todorov ;
translated by Katherine Golsan and Lucy Golsan ;
with a new afterword by the author.
p. cm. — (European horizons)
Includes bibliographical references and index.
ISBN 0-8032-4420-7 (cloth : alk paper) — ISBN 0-8032-9444-1 (pbk. : alk. paper)
1. Anthropology. I. Title. II. Series.
GN25 .T63 2001 301—dc21 00-055174
𝒩

TO FRANÇOIS FLAHAULT

Contents

Ω

Preface

Anthropology as it is generally practiced today is never "general." It has as its object particular societies or their culture. But the word can also be taken in its literal sense of "knowledge of man" to denote the concept of humanity that would underlie various investigations of the human sciences as well as moral or political discussions or even philosophy. It is this kind of anthropology that is at the origin of the present study.

General anthropology is situated halfway between the human sciences and philosophy. It does not seek to challenge either one but rather to act as a bridge allowing the two to join or to be an intermediary space that would facilitate an exchange of ideas. It differs from other disciplines such as psychology, sociology, or ethnology in that, rather than concentrating on the observation of one kind or aspect of human activity, it seeks to highlight the implicit definition of humankind itself, the unformulated intuitions of these sciences. It does not try to judge in advance, as we might think, the relative importance of identical and diverging characteristics of the species by giving more importance to the first and neglecting the second. The very idea of differences among societies or individuals implies qualities in common, and this communality makes comparisons and the study of differences fertile or at least possible. Such a general anthropology allows us to free ourselves of the jargon of each discipline or clique within that discipline, jargon that sometimes seems to be the sole purpose of its practitioners. In hoping to find what is common to these separate fields of study, anthropology is, at the same time, inevitably driven to search for a common language.

General anthropology is also different from what is usually called philosophy (except precisely that area named "philosophical anthropology") in that it has an empirical objective, the human being, and does not insist on the examination of principles and preliminary observations about the possibility or impossibility of knowledge, judgment, or even existence itself. It builds on observations and descriptions found in the human sciences rather than satisfying itself with ridiculing them for their philosophical naiveté. In that way anthropology is both *concrete* and *general*, and it is this duality that makes it timely today.

Understood in this way, the field of anthropology is vast. It is only to one of its areas that I would like to turn now in order to speak, not as is customarily done, about the place of the human being in society, but about the reverse, the place of society in the human being. What does the generally accepted idea that we are social beings actually mean? What are the consequences of this statement that *I* does not exist without *you*? What does it mean to the individual to be limited to a *life in common*?

Since the important thing for me was observation and not the scientific or pseudoscientific apparatus that surrounded it, I found the material for this study in varied sources. In the first chapter I attempt a short look at the history of Western philosophical thought—a look that does not pretend to take the place of thorough historical study; I use the past as illustration rather than trying to clarify its meaning. But I must point out that all my ideas are explorations of several daring hypotheses formulated some 250 years ago by Jean-Jacques Rousseau.

I have also used work done in the human sciences regarding the questions that interest me, especially in the field of psychology and psychoanalysis. But I do not see these disciplines as qualitatively superior to others, as if science were alone to provide us with truth about what is not science. Instead of a key that unlocks all doors, these disciplines seemed to me to be locks like the others, discourses to interpret, not the final meaning of all the other discourses. Among the different currents and schools that make up these disciplines today, I was most interested, on the one hand, in the psychology of the affective development of the very young child and, on the other, in relational psychoanalysis.

I have made more use than is customary of the works of writers: poets, novelists, autobiographers, and essayists. This practice deserves a longer explanation, for it can be seen as heretical both by the specialists of literature and by human science professionals. In fact, for both of them, literature has nothing to do with knowledge, or truth with songs. The former will say that as a pure game of its constitutive elements, it designates only itself, or else it deconstructs and blocks its pseudoaffirmations. As a vague reflection of the world, the latter would add, it does not allow itself to be reduced to propositions capable of being proved or disproved. One could answer their claims by saying that if literature did not teach us anything important about the human condition, no one would take the trouble to refer back at times to texts two thousand years old. And that if the truth of literature cannot be reduced to common methods of verifying, it could be that there are other kinds of verification. The truth of literary texts is not narrowly referential; it is intersubjective and consists in the adherence of readers far beyond centuries or national borders. For this reason, Sophocles and Shakespeare, Dostoevsky and Proust continue not only to fulfill our aesthetic aspirations but also our need to know and understand.

Literary thought is not only worthy of being included in the field of knowledge; it also has particular merits. What is expressed through stories or poetic forms escapes the stereotypes that dominate the thought of our own time and the vigilance of our own moral censure, which operates above all on assertions we manage to make explicit. Disagreeable truths—about us in particular or the human race in general—have a better chance of being expressed in a literary work than in a philosophic or scientific one. Literary thought does not lend itself to empirical or logical proof. This is true, but it awakens our ability to interpret symbolically, our capacity of association, whose movements, repercussions, shock waves continue long after the initial contact. This awakening is produced by an evocative use of words and by the use of stories, examples, and individual cases. In this sense, the works are more intelligent than their authors and our interpretations of these more intelligent than we are. Finally, literary works have the advantage of speaking to everyone and thus seek the greatest clarity. Why frown on one's pleasure in seeing La Rochefoucauld state clearly but without any concession to facility what some contemporary psychoanalyst proves pedantically in an abstruse discourse?

There is a last obvious source of anthropological knowledge, which deserves mentioning only because of the supposedly "objective" slant of current human sciences. This source is introspection. I would never have written about "life in common" if it had not interested me, if it had not seemed essential, and I have tried to understand the reason for this interest.

I would like to point out a special debt I owe to my friend, François Flahault. For twenty years life in common has been the most frequent subject of our conversations, and he has written several books and articles on this subject. It is impossible to say just how much of my own thought are his ideas, but I know it is a great deal, and I dedicate this essay to him to acknowledge his influence and to thank him.

LIFE IN COMMON

1   A Brief Look at the History of Thought

ANTISOCIAL TRADITIONS

As one studies the broad currents of European philosophical thought on the definition of what is human, a curious conclusion stands out. The social dimension, the very fact of life in common, is not generally conceived of as being *necessary* to human beings. This "thesis," however, is not presented as such; it is a supposition that remains unformulated and which, for this very reason, its author does not have the opportunity to argue, making it easier for us to accept. What is more, it forms the common denominator for theories that, in other respects, are at war with each other. Whatever the position one takes in these arguments, a definition of man as solitary and nonsocial is accepted.

The different versions of this asocial vision are easy to identify. Take first that of the great moralists of the classical period, who were themselves heirs of antiquity: those who set about analyzing morals rather than teaching morality. They present humanity to us as hesitating between two states. One is real life, which is also the life of our illusions. Human beings are certainly caught in the web of social relations, but out of weakness. The other state is that of our authentic life, even if we have difficulty in attaining it. Possibly there one could mix with gods, but as for other human beings, one is liberated from them. The superficial diversions of sociality are left far behind. Dealing with others is a burden to be discharged; asking approval from others is only an undesirable *vanity* that could never be tolerated by the wise man who aspires only to autarchy and self-sufficiency.

When Montaigne wanted to offer advice to his fellows, he expressed himself in this way: "Make our contentment depend on ourselves; let us cut loose from all the ties that bind us to others; let us win from ourselves the power to live really alone and to live that way at our ease."[1] "Abandon with other pleasures that which comes from the approbation of others."[2] It is possible and worthwhile to free oneself from relations with other human beings and especially from that approval we demand of them. This is the wisdom of the Stoics, which Montaigne passes on to us. La Bruyère concurs and concludes, not without regret, that "Men are sometimes unbearable to themselves."[3] Fortunately, this is not true everywhere or at all times. There are moments when man overcomes his illusions and manages to attain the self-sufficient ideal. Although Pascal's general outlook is very different, he shares the same idea of man. "We are not satisfied," he writes, "with our own life as it really is; we desire to live an imaginary life in the minds of others, and for that purpose we endeavour to shine."[4] He regretfully states that we do not know how to be self-sufficient, and it is with sadness that he observes us indulging in endless social entertainment. Sociality is the real, but the ideal, the profound truth of our nature, is solitude. Such is the first all-encompassing individualist conception that underlies our representations of human life.

But it is not the dominant one. The opposition between the ideal and the real, between solitude and sociality is usually of another kind. In fact, since the Renaissance, the association of "nature" with the "ideal" has been abandoned, and nature instead turns up in what would be called the real. This change came about simultaneously in political theory and psychology, and the same authors are responsible for it (Machiavelli and Hobbes became the standard bearers of this thinking). According to the new vulgate (although it was hardly a radical new idea: the wisdom of nations has for centuries taught us that men prey on each other), it is only

for centuries to come. In a first phase, it is presumed that all social relations sprang from praiseworthy qualities such as generosity and love of others. In other words, the opposition between solitude and sociality was seen as equivalent to the difference between self-ishness and altruism, obviously a distortion. In a second phase, the argument leaned toward disillusionment; the mask of virtue was torn away. This new conclusion is even more convincing in our eyes because it does not attempt to flatter, and we tell ourselves unconsciously that something disagreeable would never be ad-vanced unless it were true. Having rejected an idea of man that is too indulgent, we are left with the picture of a human being who is selfish and alone. Sociality is virtuous but virtue deceives us, so the truth must be that we are asocial. La Rochefoucauld is thus able to conclude: "Men would not live long in society were they not one another's dupes,"[7] and Pascal: "The association of one man with another is based upon this mutual deceit."[8] It is a mistake to think others wish us well. If we could see clearly, society would vanish!

But is this not an absurd conclusion of false premises? Moral judgment, the naming of vices and virtues, seems to have contami-nated the underlying anthropological concept. When La Roche-foucauld declares that only self-interest can produce friendship, he sees this phenomenon as an extreme proof, an even stronger rea-son, he suggests, that his maxim should apply to our other rela-tionships that seem to be less unselfish than friendship. Not only is this explanation of friendship inadequate, however—for if I subju-gated another entirely to my own interests his attachment would be of little value—but even more fundamental is the fact that the formula of La Rochefoucauld implies the existence of an autono-mous and self-centered "I" *preceding* all social life, a sort of owner who cares only about amassing wealth, as if the relations with people could be understood in referring to those that connect us with things. My relationship to others is not the product of my own self-interest; it precedes both the self-interest and the "I." There is no point in asking oneself, in Hobbesian fashion: Why do men choose to live in society? or like Schopenhauer: Where does the need for society come from? because mankind never makes this passage into communal life. The relationship precedes the isolated element. People do not live in society because of self-interest or because of virtue or because of the strength of other reasons, no matter what they might be. They do so because for them no other form of life is possible.

An almost identical concept of man is found in Kant, a great moralist but a questionable psychologist. According to Kant, the fundamental antagonism in the human species lies in "unsociable sociality," in the contradictory tendencies to both seek out and to flee from society. However, if the first tendency allows for the accomplishment of what is best in man (on the side of the ideal, the purpose of the human race, its regulating principle), the second is what is called his internal truth, his natural inclination. It is "the unsocial desire (existing concurrently with his social propensities) to force all things into compliance with his own humor; a propensity to which he naturally anticipates resistance from his consciousness of a similar spirit of resistance to others existing in himself."[9] From the individual's point of view, others are only rivals or obstacles to his own rise, so he hopes for their disappearance. Man is torn between the desire for unlimited power, not shared with others, and his inability to get along without society, a result of weakness. "A man whose happiness depends on *another* man's choice (no matter how benevolent the other may be) rightly considers himself unfortunate."[10]

This image of mankind leads Kant to a strange interpretation of the first cry of the newborn child, for is it not the natural intent of men to keep others at a distance, even if they must make war to accomplish this goal? "The inclination to freedom seems to be the reason why even a child who has just emerged from his mother's womb enters the world with loud cries, unlike any other animal; for he regards his inability to make use of his limbs as *constraint* and so immediately announces his claim to freedom."[11] If the newborn child cries, it is not to demand what is necessary for life and existence; it is to protest against his dependence in regard to others. As a Kantian subject, man is born longing for liberty.

In examining the details of the central human passion that drives each man to grasp power and to control others, Kant distinguishes three modalities, depending on the subject to which it applies: *Ehrsucht*, *Herrschsucht*, *Habsucht*, a thirst for honors, for domination, for possessions. However, even if this last kind can easily fit into the economic model of the accumulation of wealth, and if the second sees all other human beings as potential servants, the passion for honors is not so easily defined. The very nature of honors requires that they be accorded to us by others, by those who have the means to do so. These others cannot therefore be reduced to the role of rivals or obstacles, who, like us, aspire to the same distinctions. Here, the other is both irreducibly different from oneself and complementary. But is it not the same for many other social relationships, from friendship to apprenticeship, and even that of the newborn to his mother?

La Rochefoucauld, too, frightened by the excessive application of his defining principle, hurried to clarify it in his "Note to the Reader" in the second edition of his *Maxims*: "The word *self-interest* does not always mean an interest in the good: more often it is a desire for honor or glory."[12] This observation is profoundly true, but it removes much of the radical meaning of the initial statement. If the guiding motivation of human activity is not the acquisition of goods similar to material wealth, to selfish satisfaction, but is instead a desire for glory and honors, how can we get along without others, who are the sole purveyors possible? La Rochefoucauld is only interested in our social drives, yet he suggests that man first and foremost is a solitary being. We cannot get along without others but only because of our own selfish ambitions. However, the particular cases imagined by both La Rochefoucauld and Kant threaten their own general frame of interpretation, especially since this frame has never been explicitly confirmed. Without such a frame, who could believe that rivalry or submission exhausts the variety of human relations?

This first version of the conception, which sees man as selfish and alone, positions one on the side of morality (one must overcome natural tendencies, Kant teaches). A second version, dating from the eighteenth century at the latest, suggests that one pattern the ideal on the real rather than contrast the two; the psychological concept, however, is not modified by this choice. This position would often be taken by the materialists-encyclopedists Helvetius, Diderot, d'Holbach and, in a more outrageous fashion, Sade. In *Essays on the Mind and Its Several Faculties*, Helvetius agrees with La Rochefoucauld that self-interest governs man's conduct, but unlike his predecessor, he does not regret this fact. Diderot adopts this doctrine and adds: "What makes a man what he is . . . [is] the code of morality appropriate to men."[13] In other words, the ideal must submit to the real. And Sade concludes, "For a bridle have nothing but your inclinations, for laws only your desires, for morality Nature's alone."[14]

Nietzsche might well criticize his seventeenth- and eighteenth-century predecessors, but he shares their idea of man's nature. He has only contempt for his bourgeois contemporaries, who have lost all interest in fame and excellence and are content to live warmly and with full stomachs. But his own ideal, the Superman, is also a being who longs for solitude. In the place of the pride and selfishness of La Rochefoucauld comes the "morality of the master" with the will to power at its center. "My idea is that every specific body strives to become master over all space and to extend its force (—its will to power:) and to thrust back all that resists its extension. But it continually encounters similar efforts on the part of other bodies and ends by coming to an arrangement ("union") with those of them that are sufficiently related to it: this they then conspire together for power."[15] The human being, no different from other living creatures, wants to dominate. Others, who are all the same, are only rivals or perhaps become collaborators if the task is too big for one man alone. The best succeed. "The rich and living want victory, opponents overcome, the overflow of the feeling of power across wider domains than hitherto."[16]

Nietzsche had a strangely egalitarian psychology: All men are alike and compete for the same place; therefore, they are either my adversaries or my collaborators or, in case of victory, the defeated, my servants. Everything happens as if—assuming we are able to overcome the limitations imposed on us by a conventional morality designed to protect the weak, a morality of sheep—we were all going to rush to rule as solitary masters. But is this really the common pattern of human conduct? Is there no anguish in being a tyrant?

Here the role of the ideas of honor and glory are worth our attention. They imply a necessary reference to social life, and, moreover, they are constantly found in reflections on man among ancient as well as modern philosophers. It is equally noteworthy, however, that, in spite of profound changes in attitudes, the desire for honors and glory is always considered optional, a desire one can well do without. For the ancient philosophers it brought out the best in man; Achilles preferred death to a life without brilliance. But even so, this virtue is not present in everyone, only in the best. It is an ideal but not a basic need.

On the other hand, for modern philosophers beginning with Hobbes, the desire for glory and honor is the source of our troubles. We must learn to tame it, to consider more essential interests first: Social tranquility is worth more than the glory of heroes. The philosophers of the Enlightenment, Montesquieu and Kant, deplored our desire for glory, this uncontrollable passion, an outmoded survival of the feudal code. They also believed that man could well do without glory, but only the best would succeed at doing so. Thus when Hobbes or La Rochefoucauld propose a positive sociality as the remedy for our basic selfishness, they do not include the desire for glory and honors, which has now come to be seen as a selfish desire to be eliminated. *Ehrsucht* has no place except in the series of *Habsucht* and *Herrschsucht;* it is now only a kind of "selfish self-centeredness." (Nietzsche, on the other hand, deplored the modern decline of a desire for glory as yet another proof of the mediocrity propagated by the new democracies). In modern times the individual is encouraged to see to his own affairs, to worry about his personal development rather than to exhaust himself in useless pursuit of prestige—as if the self could exist without reference to the outside world, as if vanity and self-centeredness shared the entire field of intersubjectivity.

DISCOVERY AND ITS REDUCTION

It would certainly be misleading to say that this asocial vision corresponds to all the conceptions of man in the Western psychological tradition. This vision is clearly dominant, but it is not the only one. We can observe the "solitary" tendencies of classical philosophy, but it also has "social" tendencies. Even if autarchy remains the ideal of the wise man, the Greek philosophers believed also that man is a social animal, that he must live with his fellows and flourishes in the polis. The tension between these two affirmations is often resolved by the acceptance of several "lifestyles," all praiseworthy, even if they too can be hierarchized, permitting both active or practical life, accessible to all, and taking place in society, and a contemplative, solitary life, particularly suitable to the wise. Even while acknowledging the fundamental fact of human plurality, however, the Greek philosophers usually do not see "you" as different from "I" and necessary to wholeness; they do not explore the difference of position between "I" and "other." The natural sympathy that exists between men is that of like for like. Others are necessary so that virtue can manifest itself (Aristotle: "for us, well-being has reference to something other than ourselves"[17]), not because each particular subject would be incomplete without others. Friendship also is a merit rather than a need. Cicero is even more explicit: "Nature gave us friendship as an aid to virtue . . .

since virtue when solitary cannot arrive at the highest kind of life, it might do so when joined and shared with a companion."[18]

Aristotle also left us this well-known formula: "But he who is unable to live in society, or who has no need because he is sufficient for himself, must be either a beast or a god."[19] Animals and gods are self-sufficient and therefore can be seen as alone. Man is irremediably incomplete; he needs others. It is clear, however, that these others are necessary as a natural environment for the individual, not in order to assume any particular function. The relation that Aristotle envisions is the copresence of individuals at the heart of the polis, not the complementarity of the seer and the seen. In the myth of Aristophanes recounted by Plato in *The Symposium*, human beings need "[the] other half"[20] (*symbolon*) of the other being and are thus intrinsically incomplete. But this complementarity explains sexual attraction rather than the foundation of a communal life: the fit of the male sexual organ in the female becomes the image of desired completeness. Plato himself postulates the presence of ardor, *thymos*, as one of the components of the soul, and represents it as attached to the passion for honors, to the love of triumph, but he does not state that only others can bestow this reward. And the Stoics note that vanity is omnipresent but think that man can liberate himself from it.

Disregarding for a moment several early signs of what was to come, one can say that a real revolution took place in the middle of the eighteenth century, when Jean-Jacques Rousseau became the first to formulate a new conception of man as a being who *needs others*. One must note, however, that two traits of Rousseau's discourse have confused his message slightly and have sometimes prevented its meaning from being understood. The first difficulty is that Rousseau's philosophical anthropology, offered in *Discourse on the Origin of Inequality*, takes the form of a historical account while, at the same time, he warns us against any projection of his mental constructs onto history. The "state of nature" that he imagines, as he announces from the beginning of the *Discourse*, is "a state which no longer exists, which perhaps never did exist, which probably never will exist, and about which it is nevertheless necessary to have exact Notions in order accurately to judge of our present state."[21] It is very difficult to constantly keep in mind that the first "stages" of humanity imagined by Rousseau come only from "hypothetical and conditional reasoning," and that the only real humanity is the present one.

The second difficulty arises from the fact that Rousseau the man was dominated by a touchy and suspicious temperament, that he believed himself persecuted and therefore often preferred solitude to company—a solitude even more desirable then than now since it was much harder to come by. But in Rousseau's mind this personal preference for isolation does not correspond to a doctrinal affirmation of man's essential aloneness. He carefully underlines the distance between the general rule (the recommendations he gives to Emile) and the exception (his own destiny). And in the *Dialogues*, after having advised us of his own preference for solitude, he insists on reminding us: "Absolute solitude is a state that is sad and contrary to nature."[22] Therefore, it is first necessary to remove the veil that obscures our perception of Rousseau's thought, and then all of his audaciousness will be revealed.

Rousseau does accompany those I have called "moralists" (in the tradition of Montaigne) part of the way in condemning life in society and in presenting the solitude of an individual in a favorable light. To do so, he used a distinction in terminology between *amour de soi*, or self-love, and *amour-propre*, or vanity. The first notion is positive; it is the simple instinct of self-preservation, indispensable for every human. Although it precedes moral attitudes, it is still identified with virtues (and, modified by pity, it will form the basis for these) and not selfishness. The second notion is considered negative by Rousseau. It is a feeling that exists only in society and consists in comparing ourselves to others, in judging ourselves superior to them, and in wanting them to be inferior. Rousseau's *amour-propre* is not that of La Rochefoucauld, where this idea is mixed with "self-love." It corresponds more to what the other moralists call vanity; it is our dependence on the opinion of others. "*Amour-propre*, which is to say a relative feeling [this term in Rousseau is a synonym for "social"] by which one makes comparisons; the latter feeling demands preferences, whose enjoyment is purely negative, and it no longer seeks satisfaction in our own benefit but solely in the harm of another."[23]

If Rousseau's argument stopped here, he would be no more than a sworn opponent—particularly virulent and eloquent—of human vanity and of the desire to surpass others. The human relations he envisions here, as in the other moralists, still come from similarity—we compare ourselves to others, we would like to take the place of the other, we fight our rivals. The entire question now is whether this type of relationship exhausts the whole social field, as Rousseau's predecessors suggested in basing their condemnation of life in society on it, or if other relationships exist that are equally social but no longer spring from similarity and therefore do not lead to comparisons or the desire to replace or rival another.

Rousseau's merit is precisely to have envisaged this other type of social relationship and to have anticipated its effect on human identity, even though the term he uses for it is not generally comparable to self-love or to *amour-propre*. This third feeling, halfway between the other two, is "the idea of consideration."[24] Ever since human beings have lived in society (which, in regard to historical time, means always), they have felt the need to attract the gaze of others. The specifically human organ is the eyes. "Everyone began to look at everyone else and to wish to be looked at himself."[25] The other no longer occupies a position comparable to mine but contiguous and complementary; he is necessary to my own completeness. The effects of this need resemble those of vanity. We want to be looked at, we search for public recognition, we try to interest others in our fate. This desire differs from vanity in that it is a basic need of the species as we know it and not a vice. The innovation of Rousseau is not that he stated that men can be moved by a desire for glory or prestige—all the moralists knew this—but that he made this desire the threshold on this side of which we cannot really speak of humanity. The need to be recognized, the need for recognition are human properties discovered by Rousseau that can reach far beyond a desire for honor.

Sociability is not an accident or a contingency; it is the very definition of the human condition. We understand now the solemnity of tone that Rousseau chooses in the *Essay on the Origin of Languages*. "He who willed man to be sociable inclined the globe's axis at an angle to the axis of the universe with a touch of the finger. With this slight motion I see the face of the earth change and the vocation of mankind settled."[26] But this "vocation" means that we have a pressing need of others, not to satisfy our vanity, but because, marked by an original incompleteness, we owe others our very existence. Elsewhere Rousseau writes: "Every attachment is a sign of insufficiency. If each of us had no need of others, he would hardly think of uniting himself with them."[27] But we are that way: born incomplete, dying incomplete, always the prey of others' needs, always in quest of the missing complement. Only God knows happiness in solitude. Here Rousseau rejoins Aristotle's thinking as he accepts the idea that society is born of the weakness of the individual. His essential contribution, however, is in the insistence that man brings to existence an innate insufficiency and that, therefore, each of us has a real need of others, a need to be *considered*, a "need to attach his heart."[28]

What makes man feel his own existence? Sometimes Rousseau uses this expression as an equivalent of self-love and of the instinct for self-preservation. When he introduces the perspective of sociability, however, he places it—as he should—within the "idea of consideration."[29] He reaches this conclusion in *Discourse on the Origins of Inequality*. "The Savage lives within himself; sociable man, [but that means, let us remember, man as he actually exists] always outside himself, is capable of living only in the opinion of others and, so to speak, derives the sentiment of his own existence solely

13

from their judgement."[30] Rousseau confirms this point of view in the *Dialogues*. A human being is distinguished from animals because he has, in addition to his physical sensibility (which serves his survival instinct), a social sensibility, "the faculty of attaching our affections to beings who are foreign to us."[31] The exercise of this faculty serves "to extend and reinforce the feeling of our being."[32] The relationship to another enlarges the self rather than reducing it. This characteristic of man makes him what he is; it is the source of his virtues and his vices, of his unending misfortunes and his frail happiness.

By thus inscribing a need for the gaze of the other in the very definition of man, Rousseau parts company with the classical tradition, even though the different ingredients of his doctrine could already be found there. If we set aside his genius, what allowed him to take this decisive step in the understanding of the human condition? Perhaps, as Charles Taylor suggests, the historical context plays a part. In the middle of the eighteenth century, the old system of honors, reserved for a few of the privileged, began to fall into disuse; everyone hoped for public recognition, what one would call dignity. What had once been accepted without question became a problem and was brought out into the open. Rousseau would be among the first to perceive the change. His contribution, however, goes far beyond what one finds in analyzing only the historical context.

It is not possible here to trace in every detail the later effects of Rousseau's discovery, but two reactions, close to each other in time, are worth recalling, for they show both the reverberation of the discovery and its diversity.

The first can be found in the work of the Scottish philosopher and economist, Adam Smith. At barely thirty years of age, Smith was teaching moral philosophy at Glasgow when Rousseau's work appeared. Smith immediately became acquainted with it and wrote an insightful review in 1756. What he admired especially in Rousseau was the importance of pity and therefore of sociality. He was delighted to find an ally in the struggle against the asocial theories of Hobbes, La Rochefoucauld, and Mandeville. Smith thought the Hobbesian view did not take sympathy into account, which was the cornerstone of his own system and which he defined broadly as our ability to share the feelings of others whatever they might be, and whose existence can be confirmed by the everyday experience of each of us.

When he published *Theory of Moral Sentiments* in 1759, Smith did not refer openly to Rousseau, but the primary thesis of *Discourse on the Origins of Inequality*—the idea that our accession to humanity consists in the acknowledgment we accord each other—plays a central role, especially in explaining the motivations of human actions. What is the goal one pursues in life, what makes up this improvement of our condition that we all hope for? "To be observed, to be attended to, to be taken notice of with sympathy, complacency, and approbation, are all the advantages which we can propose to derive from it."[33] That we are taken into consideration by others is both "the most agreeable hope" and "the most ardent desire of human nature."[34] No one except the perfect wise man and the man reduced to the level of an animal can remain indifferent to the attraction of public recognition. There is no price we are not prepared to pay to obtain it, for "men have voluntarily thrown away life to acquire after death a renown which they could no longer enjoy"[35] (a classic example of the superiority of passions over self-interest).

The absence of esteem, on the other hand, is the worst evil that could befall us: "Compared with the contempt of mankind, all other external evils are easily supported."[36] The great men of this world are "observed by all the world,"[37] and their unhappiness, always a threat, would consist in no longer being "surrounded by that admiring mob of fools, flatterers and dependants,"[38] to no longer be "gazed upon by the multitude."[39] Smith's description of our dependence on others is full of visual terms: show, hide, notice, look, observe, ignore, consideration, sight, eyes, attention, gaze.

The need to be acknowledged is not just one human motivation among others; it is the truth behind all other needs. Material riches are not an end in themselves but a way for us to be assured of the recognition of others. "It is chiefly from this regard to the sentiments of mankind, that we pursue riches and avoid poverty."[40] The rich man is happy because he has managed to draw the attention of the world even though he may later try to camouflage his wealth. It is the same with pleasures: the ones we feel the most intensely are those we receive from the special attention others pay us. "Nature, when she formed man for society, . . . taught him to feel pleasure in their favorable and pain in their unfavorable regard."[41] Other pleasures are unimportant compared to this one. "It is not ease or pleasure, but always honour, of one kind or another . . . that the ambitious man really pursues."[42] It follows, as Jean-Pierre Dupuy has noted in his commentary on Smith, that "the subject imagined by Smith is radically incomplete,"[43] because he cannot do without the attention of others. "He is desperately in need of his fellowmen to forge an identity for himself."[44] In this sense, Smith is a disciple of Rousseau.

Honor is not integrated here, as it will be later by Kant, into an undifferentiated series of desires (of possessions, of power, of honor). Understood in its larger sense as referring to the attention and the judgment of others, it is the true root of other desires. Here Smith has the merit of overcoming an opposition, transmitted from century to century, between our prideful aspirations, on the one hand, and utilitarian ones, on the other, or as Albert Hirschman has put it, between passions and interests. We know that such a distribution has often been dreamed of: place on the right everything men do for "good" reasons, for example, enriching themselves, and on the left all their follies, the search for fame, fidelity to symbols. Adam Smith suggests, however, that these apparent oppositions are only diverse ways of arriving at the same end. "Smith refuses to be taken in by the falseness of bourgeois individualism or selfish interests,"[45] Dupuy concludes. On this very point Adam

Smith went one step further than Rousseau, who, as we have seen, attributed self-love to all living beings but the idea of recognition of others and its perversion, *amour-propre*, only to human beings. Smith abandoned completely the idea of an autonomous self-love in man. *Amour-propre* is the truth of self-love; the selfish accumulation of wealth is only a way of assuring the recognition of others.

Judging by these last examples, one could think that Adam Smith brings a negative judgment to this dependence of human beings on the recognition of others, but he does not. The human condition must be accepted as it is. This conclusion in no way prevents Smith from distinguishing between vice and virtue. Like Rousseau, who separates *amour-propre* from "the idea of recognition," he does not confuse vanity with the interdependence of men, which is exactly what he reproaches La Rochefoucauld and Mandeville for doing. They first erase any difference between the recognition demanded in order to claim that self-interest alone governs our actions. Mandeville "treats every thing as vanity which has any reference, either to what are, or to what ought to be the sentiments of others."[46] But the desire for fame is not to be confused with vanity, or the desire to be good with the pleasure of receiving compliments.

The human passions that push us toward each other are, therefore, not reprehensible in themselves. That which can become a source of corruption is, at the point of departure, necessary to life in society, to human life. We must even thank "the all-wise Author of Nature" who, in this manner, has "taught man to respect the sentiments and judgments of his brethren," and who has "made man, if I may say so, the immediate judge of human nature,"[47] for the source of all judgment is in reference to another. Just as for Rousseau, for Adam Smith all values, ethical as well as aesthetic, can only come about in society. We cannot make a judgment of ourselves without stepping outside of ourselves and seeing through the eyes of others. If a human being could be brought up in isolation, he would be unable to judge anything, not even himself, for the mirror to see himself would be lacking. "Bring him into society, and he is immediately provided with the mirror which he wanted before."[48] Montaigne, it is true, was already speaking of himself in these terms: "Training myself from my youth to see my own life mirrored in that of others."[49]

Does this mean we must bend all our efforts toward a positive judgment from others? We also know that this judgment can be volatile and superficial. If God existed, we could depend on his clairvoyance and give up trying to evaluate mankind. In the strictly human world of Adam Smith, however, this eventuality is not taken into consideration. What Smith suggests instead is a mental construct, available to everyone, of an "impartial and well-informed spectator"[50] who lives within us, an ideal model of all the "others" that we meet in life (which, in the twentieth century, George Herbert Mead would call "the generalized other" and Mikhail Bakhtin, the "super addressee"). This spectator is exclusively human and at the same time free of the faults unique to each of us. It allows us to avoid being arrogant and still look for recognition by others.

This impartial and enlightened spectator is not just a fiction of the philosopher: we all possess such an ideal representation within us, which we call *conscience,* and which is, in reality, nothing but a generalized other, the gaze of the other within us; it is on the judgment of this generalized other that our conduct finally depends. Those who, full of good intentions, present the human being as acting out of love for humanity, deceive themselves just as much as those who, motivated in this case by a pitiless love of truth, deal us a blow by insisting that man acts only at the bidding of his selfish interests. Man cannot satisfy himself alone, but he does not necessarily obey a duty that he sees as imposed by the community. "It is not the love of our neighbor, it is not the love of mankind, which upon many occasions prompts us to the practice of those divine virtues. It is a stronger love, a more powerful affection, which generally takes place upon such occasions, the love of what is honourable and noble, of the grandeur, dignity, and superiority of our own characters."[51] The most powerful motives of human action are not named pleasure, self interest, greed, or, on the other side, generosity, love of humanity, self-sacrifice, but rather a desire for glory and recognition, shame and guilt, fear of a lack of esteem, a need of recognition, a call for the attention of others.

Adam Smith accepted and developed Rousseau's intuition without betraying it, an entirely different treatment from that which it received at the hands of Hegel. As an admirer and reader of both Rousseau and Adam Smith, Hegel tackled the problem of the makeup of our sociality in the famous pages of *Phenomenology of Mind* (1807), which was devoted to the "dialectic of the master and servant," (or the slave), pages I will read, as did so many before me, in the interpretation proposed by Alexandre Kojève in the 1930s (*Introduction to the Reading of Hegel*). Kojève's interpretation does not correspond exactly to the original for, like any interpreter, Kojève reorients and transforms the text he is reading. This interpretation, however, has the advantage of being much more explicit than the original. The reorientations are, moreover, partly those projected onto Hegel from the nineteenth century. In many respects the world reacted to Hegelian thought as though it conformed to Kojève's interpretation.

Actually, Hegel (who in these pages of *Phenomenology* does not refer to either Rousseau or Adam Smith) interprets and changes Rousseau's thought in two directions. On the one hand, he forcefully expands and affirms it. Rather than keep the "idea of recognition" as a transitory state between self-love and *amour-propre* and pride, he makes it the main characteristic of the human species. And rather than condemning it as pride, arrogance, or vanity, he describes it in morally neutral terms. What does the difference between animal and man actually consist of? The former acts in accordance with its instinct for preservation and to this end takes over the necessities (for example, food) and removes the obstacles (the rivals). The latter acts in the same way but is not satisfied with material satisfaction alone; man wants recognition of his value, which can come only from the acknowledgment of others. Recognition (*Anerkennung*) will be the term Hegel uses for what Rousseau called "consideration," and Adam Smith "attention." It is this last term I intend to use myself.

The human being begins when the "*biological* desire to preserve his *life*," bows to "the *human* desire for *Recognition*."[52] "Human Desire, therefore, must win out over this desire for preservation. In other words, man's humanity 'comes to light' only if he risks his (animal) life for the sake of his human Desire."[53] As Adam Smith has already reminded us, man is prepared to lose his life to become renowned. Achilles, who preferred glory to life, was the first authentic representative of humanity and not just a great hero. The need for recognition is the fundamental human fact. It is in this sense that man does not exist before society and that the human being is rooted in interhuman relationships. "Human reality can only be social." "If they are to be *human*, they must be at least *two* in number."[54] Hegel did not have the personal reasons of Rousseau to deplore the human condition; he contents himself with describing it.

At the same time that he is working to establish a broader scope, however, Hegel-Kojève considerably limits the idea of recognition. This limitation is accomplished in several steps. The first begins with a severe application of the law of the excluded third. In order to go beyond being an animal, man must look not only for what satisfies him immediately and the instinct for survival but also for "something that goes beyond the given reality. Now, the only thing that goes beyond the given reality is Desire itself."[55] Or further, "To be anthropogenetic, then, Desire must be directed toward a nonbeing—that is, toward another *Desire*, another greedy emptiness, another *I*."[56] But does the world of desired objects necessarily separate itself into excluding parts, material objects, and other desires?

The second step is even more drastic. At the same time that I ask for recognition from another, he asks the same of me, something we cannot both do since one must do without it for the other to receive it. The demand for recognition must necessarily be a struggle, and since for humans recognition is a value more valuable than life itself, it is a life-and-death struggle. In fact, this idea was not absent from Rousseau (nor from other authors before him), but for him it concerned *amour-propre* (a negative), not the idea of recognition or the need of others (a neutral). He wrote: "I would show how much this universal desire for reputation, honors, and preferment which consumes us all exercises and compares talents and strengths, how much it excites and multiplies the passions and, in making all men competitors, rivals, or rather enemies, how many reverses, how many successes, how many catastrophes of every kind it daily causes by leading so many Contenders to enter the same lists."[57] Since Hegel-Kojève does not distinguish between these different characteristics (self-love, *amour-propre*), he applies this description to the idea of recognition itself. Because each of the two partners is prepared to risk his life rather than to capitulate, their encounter can be only a "fight to the death for pure prestige,"[58] which would be difficult to condemn since it is a part of the definition of humanity. It is "a life and death *Fight*. A *Fight*, since each will want to subjugate the other, *all* the others, by a negating, destroying *action*."[59] To make oneself recognized is to impose oneself on the other. Thus the idea of recognition finds itself unfailingly attached to that of the struggle for power.

This second step was, in its turn, prepared for by a third reduction, which interprets all recognition as that of a value. In the Hegel-Kojève vocabulary, recognition is a value, a synonym of admiration and approval, of praise, and therefore in an inferior position to something superior. "Now, all Desire is desire for a value."[60]

Finally, a last reduction in reasoning is made by Hegel-Kojève when he imagines the consequences of this original confrontation.

One of the two combatants has emerged the winner of the conflict; the other has been beaten and, if he has not been killed, becomes the slave or servant (he prefers to save his own life than to crave recognition). But in doing so he gives up his specifically human condition. As for the winner, he is frustrated in his turn. He receives recognition certainly but not from another *man*, which is the recognition he had hoped for. His desire is intrinsically tragic, for either he does not receive recognition because he is beaten or what he does receive is without value because it comes from the beaten man. The master "is recognized by someone whom he does not recognize. . . . The master's attitude, therefore, is an existential impasse."[61]

Here we realize not only that all demand is a struggle for recognition, but also that all struggle is a demand for recognition. Victory brings no satisfaction because it cannot be crowned by an admiring recognition, and when Hegel-Kojève declares that "there must be at least two," he also means to say "and only two." In this scenario the world is inhabited at any given moment by only a winner and a loser. Here again, we can doubt the legitimacy of such a reduction. Certainly the SS officer who killed or made slaves of those detained in concentration camps could not enjoy the pleasure of the recognition of his victims. But isn't he *at the same time* able to ask for that recognition from his SS comrades, who admire his "toughness," and from his superiors, who value his faithfulness and his willingness? To suggest this scenario, however, is to suggest that, from the very beginning, there are three and not just two actors: the two combatants and a *witness*, a *spectator* before whom the combat is played out.

The history we have from Hegel-Kojève is a parallel of Rousseau's in his *Discourse on the Origins of Inequality* and other similar writings; it is the story of the origin of humanity. What Hegel-Kojève describes for us are the first humans, the act of birth of the species, and that is why he speaks constantly of the "anthropogeny" of man "at the moment of birth," "at his origin."[62] To sum up: "Man was born and History began with the first Fight that ended in the appearance of a Master and a Slave."[63] The history of man is nothing but the evolution of this relation between masters and slaves.

The speculations on the origin of humanity familiar to philosophy until recent times belong to the source of myth. They can be very suggestive, but they are never proved or disproved. At best they furnish us with a logical model, an explanatory representation that does not need to have an existence in fact. However, it is possible to observe another birth, no longer of the species but of the individual. Even if we do not want to give it a primary role, this event remains an example of human identity as significant as any other. The two valiant combatants in Hegel-Kojève must surely have been children before becoming adults. They certainly came from their mother's womb and not the brain of a philosopher. If in reading the Hegel-Kojève myth, we keep in mind, as an illustration, the birth of the individual, many elements of the myth appear questionable if not frankly ridiculous. The model turns out to be unworkable.

Just as in the myth of the origin of the species, in the reality of the origin of the individual there must be at least two beings for the human to emerge, but these two are not, as in Hegel-Kojève, two males who face each other as if they were in a knightly tournament or a boxing ring. Instead they are a mother and child (or if you want to go back to conception, a man and a woman). The description of the origin, of birth, of the "anthropogenetic" as a life and death struggle certainly does not apply to the relationship between mother and child. Man is not born of a struggle but out of love. And the result of this birth is not the master-slave couple but, more prosaically, the parent-child couple.

One might object that the birth of offspring by man has in itself nothing specifically human. It resembles that of other mammals, even if the trace it leaves in the memory of the mother, and perhaps even in the child, has no equivalent in the animal world. The first

movements toward each other of parent and child are not specifically human either; the child "asks" to be nourished and kept
warm, in a word, protected. The mother "asks" to protect, true,
but this relationship has its equivalent in the animal world. However, at the end of several weeks a specifically human act does take
place, and it has no equivalent in other mammals. The child tries to
capture the gaze of his mother, not only so that she can come and
nourish or comfort him, but because this look in itself offers an
indispensable complement: it assures him of his existence. In other
words, the child now "asks" for the mother's recognition (or of the
adult assuming this role, who can also be the father or a third
person); the mother tries to give this recognition to her child to
assure him of his existence. At the same time, without always
recognizing it, she finds herself acknowledged in her role as the
agent of this recognition by the demanding gaze of her child. The
existence of the individual, in as much as it is specifically human,
does not begin on a battlefield but in the capturing of the maternal
gaze by the baby—a situation clearly less heroic. Let us add, in
order to avoid any misunderstanding, that the term "gaze" here
refers to the first and best of all the tools available to man for
establishing contact with another, but that in its absence—as with
the blind—the other senses, touch and hearing above all, will perform the same task.

We are now able to measure the strength of the reductions made
by Hegel-Kojève on the process of recognition in opposing them
with that which can be observed in the mother-child relationship.
First, is it legitimate to reduce all demands for nonmaterial wealth
(concretely, other than food) to another desire? Does the nursling
desire the desire of his mother? He wants her gaze, her presence, in
a word, her recognition, but strictly speaking, this cannot be called
desire except by an undue stretch of the imagination. Second, is
this demand for acknowledgment necessarily a struggle, even a
murderous one? We would have trouble accepting this proposi-

tion. Much later, a rivalry between parent and child can develop; the child can fight his father or his mother but certainly not at this initial stage. The idea of a struggle is quite distant from the thoughts of both. The child does not fight his parent; he seeks him or her out. The inequality between the child and the parent is such that in the beginning it would be absurd to imagine that the relationship could evolve *toward* inequality; the hierarchy guards against conflict. In demanding the recognition of the other (the mother), the child does not actually run any risk, but he does loudly confirm his humanity. Third, the child does not demand confirmation of his value (he does not know what it is); he is content to demand the acknowledgment of his existence, nothing more (a demand that is already enormous).

Finally, in the fourth step in the process of individual development, we notice that the conflictual relationships are not always accompanied by a demand for recognition (no more than the reverse). The conflicts are rather made up of triangular situations in which, in addition to the rivals, there is also a witness, a judge, a possessor of recognition. Therefore, the two processes, recognition and combat, can take place independently. Another proof of the possibility of dissociating the two processes comes from the observation of animals (which was in an early stage of development in Hegel's time). Animals living in packs conform rather closely to the Hegelian schema of combat leading to mastery or slavery. Rivals engage in fights to the death, but they too can get out of them by giving the winner signs of submission. Incidentally, this shows that risking one's life to win domination does not yet allow us to be part of the human category. A study, already old, explains how social life is carried out in the chicken coop. At first, there are conflicts and later submission. Should we conclude from this study that human society is nothing but a vast chicken coop? No, because in this instance combat takes place without any demand for recognition; it is a pure test of strength. Furthermore, life in the chicken coop is in no way reduced to it. With animals, as with men, it is not conflict that is the primary social relationship; it is filiation.

Can the parent-child connection be assimilated by that of the master-slave? This proposition can hardly be supported. Should we identify the child with the slave (because he is inferior) or with the master (because he demands and receives recognition)? To mix the two relationships would not only be useless, but in doing so, we would also lose the possibility of observing that *certain* parent-child relations, at *certain* moments of evolution, can actually be part of the master-slave logic.

A conclusion is in order. The Hegel-Kojève description, as brilliant as it is, does not reveal the truth about the human condition. Instead, it describes a very special relationship of a desire frustrated in its own realization, of the rivalry accompanied by the paradoxical demand for recognition on the part of the rival. It is not false, but the pretension it makes to universality is exorbitant. The reality of human relationships is infinitely richer. Everything that is not material is not desire. All recognition is not struggle for power nor a demand for confirmation of a value; every struggle is not accompanied by a demand for recognition. The human world is much more polymorphic than the "dialectic of master and slave" put forth by Hegel-Kojève would have us believe. It is also difficult to subscribe to the Hegelian conclusion, "human, historical, self-conscious existence is possible only where there are, or—at least—where there have been, bloody fights, wars for prestige."[64] The extraordinary diversity of demands and the bestowing of recognition finds itself here reduced to the monotony of a conflict over power. Its exploration hardly begun, recognition is seen reduced to only one of its varieties and almost identical with this other tired tenant of Western philosophy, a permanent war of everyone against everyone else. It is this self-mutilating limitation that needs to be overcome today.

MODERN SURVIVALS

It is obviously impossible to take in at a glance all the different theories that in our own century have claimed to rediscover Rousseau's work and have tried to transform or to contradict it. One may say, however, that the most influential doctrines seem to be prolongations of earlier asocial tendencies, those of Hobbes or La Rochefoucauld or Helvetius or, even more, Hegel's reinterpretation (and reduction) of Rousseau, a version that, well before Kojève's interpretation, had become essential to Western thought as much by way of Marxism, which translated the master and slave dialectic into a pitiless struggle between classes, as by Nietzsche's idea of the will to power. A few examples can illustrate this situation without claiming to substitute for a systematic description.

Mainstream psychoanalysis, the school of thought that today has almost completely eliminated its rivals in the field of psychological theory, often rejoins the concepts of La Rochefoucauld and Kant in stating that man is self-centered and basically solitary, that he thinks only of satisfying his desires, and that it is life in society that teaches him altruism and generosity, which are ideals and not reality. The deepest drives concern only the interests of the subject himself. In this regard, Freud shares the ideas of his illustrious predecessors, which were particularly popular in the nineteenth century. In *Civilization and Its Discontents*, he writes, "*Homo homini lupus*. Who, in the face of all his experience of life and of history, will have the courage to dispute this assertion? . . . when the mental counter-forces which ordinarily inhibit it are out of action, it also manifests itself spontaneously and reveals man as a savage beast to whom consideration towards his own kind is something alien."[65] This savage beast (but where have we seen beasts act in this way?) acknowledges others only in the measure that they will allow him to satisfy certain drives, as a sexual object or perhaps as a helper in accomplishing an especially difficult task. Otherwise, all are rivals.

The aggressive and competitive being is, therefore, essentially solitary, isolated, autarchic.

From this perspective, society is presented as a remedy to offset the inconveniences of a permanent war of all against all. It is on the side of morality and civilization, and it is artificial. "It is impossible to overlook the extent to which civilization is built up upon a renunciation of instinct, how much it presupposes precisely the non-satisfaction (by suppression, repression or some other means?) of powerful instincts. This 'cultural frustration' dominates the large field of social relationships between human beings."[66] There is, therefore, a permanent conflict between civilization and savagery (which would be the satisfaction of our drives). "In consequence of this primary mutual hostility of human beings, civilized society is perpetually threatened with disintegration."[67] Nature is made up of individual instincts. Life in society is a cultural acquisition; therefore the individual exists prior to his entry into society. Kant declared this proposition to be true. "In this way arise the first steps from the savage state to the state of culture, which consists peculiarly in the social worth of man."[68] Each time the social is reduced to the virtuous—which is missing in natural man.

The underlying concept of the human being as an individual originally isolated explains several of the most influential theses of Freudian doctrine. For example, it provides the basis for the theory of a primary narcissism. As Michael Balint has shown, Freud remained hesitant on this point in postulating "at the origin" sometimes an object relation (therefore with others), sometimes an autoeroticism, sometimes narcissism. In his definitive synthesis, however, and thus also in the psychoanalytic orthodoxy, it is agreed that the primitive state of man is characterized by "the total absence of any relationship to the outside world." It is a rigorously "objectless" state.[69] The libido is in the beginning entirely reserved for the subject itself, and only little by little is the narcissistic libido transformed into an object libido. Another example of this same underground action of Freudian anthropology is seen in the decisive role that the founder of psychoanalysis gives to the "Oedipus complex," in which the desire of the subject is inextricably linked to relationships of rivalry and hate. This articulation has always been considered by Freud and the orthodox psychoanalysts as the principal line of reference in the evolution of the individual as well as the species, since the murder of the primitive father is considered, in *Totem and Taboo*, as the original moment of humanity. Everything that cannot be reduced to the Oedipus receives the name of "preoedipal," which prepares the coming of the decisive moment. As Hegel did, Freud postulates that in the beginning was war, a struggle to the death.

It is instructive to observe the repetition of this schema in a dissenting disciple of Freud's such as Alfred Adler, who would prefer to present a more "social" portrait of man than that of classical psychoanalysis. His case is interesting. On the one hand, we find in Adler the thesis of the solitary-and-selfish man, one he often expresses in a Nietzschean vocabulary. Every human being is dominated by an "intensive striving for power,"[70] and his only goal is "achieving the mastery of the external world."[71] Life is nothing more than a "struggle for superiority"[72] and "the goal of superiority, of power, of the conquest of others, is the goal which directs the activity of most human beings."[73] Therefore, in this perspective, others are only rivals to eliminate or potential servants.

At the same time, Adler is attentive to another facet of human behavior (he is perhaps influenced here by his socialist convictions): acts of cooperation that do not arise from rivalry and that cannot be reduced to group plots against a superior. Thus it is with the newborn's movement toward the breast of the mother, which he does not want to interpret, as Kant did, as an affirmation of liberty, but neither, following Freud, as an act of aggression. "Hence, it is easy to understand that the first act of a new-born child—drinking from the mother's breast—is co-operation, and is as pleasant for the mother as for the child. It is not cannibalism or a proof of inherited sadistic instincts, as Freud, bolstering up his preconceived theory, imagines."[74] In a more general way, when he studies the behavior of women (Adler also has feminist convictions), he does not find any confirmation of his theories on the thirst for power. "The insecurity of life has not until now—and in a general way—found any other solution than a search for power. It is time for reflection about whether this is the only, the best road to a secure life and for the development of mankind. There is also something to learn about the structure of a woman's life."[75] Finally, reflecting on the history of humanity, he cannot avoid finding that one is never dealing with an isolated individual. "The communal life of man antedates the individual life of man," he wrote in *Understanding Human Nature*, and in *Social Interest:* "No isolated persons are to be found in the whole history of humanity."[76]

But how can we reconcile two such divergent claims? Here Adler offers nothing new either. It is the distinction between real and ideal that allows him to carry out the miraculous articulation. Rivalry is natural; cooperation is cultural (he forgets that with other mammals the infant also nurses at the mother's breast and that animals also practice collaboration). A passage from *Understanding Human Nature* clarifies in this way the extent of the preceding observation. "In the history of human civilization no form of life whose foundations were not laid communally can be found. No human being ever appeared except in a community of human beings."[77] In the same way, the relationship of mother and child represents not the embryo of all human life but the prototype of *civilization*. "We probably owe to the maternal sense of contact the largest part of human social feeling, and along with it the essential continuance of human civilization."[78] (Here Adler picks up the ideas of Bachofen, also familiar to but disputed by Freud.)

Adler sees human life as dominated by two conflicting movements: on one side, the thirst for power, the hope of superiority, on the other, the feeling of human communion; on one side, solitude, on the other, sociality; on one side, (bad) nature, on the other, (good) culture; evil self-centeredness and good altruism. All the effort of Adler, educator and therapist, would therefore consist of pushing us toward an acceptance of a feeling of human community, the *Mitmenschlichkeit*, a word that summarizes his ideal. Although it is impossible to verify its absence, society is not natural to man but a remedy for the original weakness of the individual. Man "is not strong enough to live alone," and out of this—here Adler repeats Rousseau—comes "the necessity of that communal life."[79]

Adler does not realize that his two directions of the psyche are both social, but one of them operates on relations of similarity, the other on those of contiguity and complementarity ("symmetric" and "asymmetric" relations). Further, he does not like to imagine a "bad" sociality (nonvirtuous), but he is forced to do so in mentioning vanity, where he takes on the tone of moralists in the tradition of Montaigne. "[H]ow unhealthy vanity can be for the social feeling."[80] But is vanity anything other than a wild pursuit of recognition, which the attention of others can give us, a perfect social sentiment?

One of the principal contributions of Adler to psychological theory concerns the identification of the description of the "feeling of inferiority," which can eventually become an "inferiority complex." Here we find the same contradictions and dead ends in his general theory. What are we talking about? Adler's opinion is that this feeling would be characteristic of the child, for, like every human creature, the child is dominated by a "striving to express power over the environment."[81] However, at this age it is impossible: "Since every child must grow up in an environment of adults he is predisposed to consider himself weak, small, incapable of living alone."[82] Eventually, organic malformations are added to this general reason for weakness, all of these factors contributing to the feeling of inferiority taking root within us, a feeling that does not lessen, if it ever does, before we arrive at adulthood and also at power, even if this feeling is tempered by a feeling of human communion.

A child, however, does not suffer from the superiority of its parents; we have only to observe the child to verify this fact. It is the adolescent who may suffer from a hierarchical superiority for which he finds no justification. The child may have this feeling toward his brothers and sisters or his playmates. But he demands something quite different from his parents: to be recognized by their gaze and their words, and he wants to imitate, rather than to combat, them. Just as the newborn needs others (his mother) in order to live, the child needs others (his parents) in order to exist, that is, to be conscious of himself through being recognized by others. Even when he tells his parents: "I'm the strongest!" the child is not looking for superiority over them but rather recognition of his existence and confirmation of his value, something only others can give him and which is much more important than victory over a rival. By interpreting the relationship of complementarity characteristic of the parent-child relationship in terms of a rivalry and thus of similarity, Adler projects onto the world of childhood a situation frequently (but not generally) obtaining among adults.

When he takes up particular cases, however, Adler betrays his own theory. Describing the spoiled child, he tells us that the child tries to "sun himself in the love of his parents," to "fix their attention on himself," to "leave no stone unturned until he occupies the limelight and has achieved more importance than any one else,"[83] and so on. What has happened to the thirst for power and the desire for superiority? However, the accurate observations of these traits cannot rise to theoretical formulation. The chosen conceptual framework leaves no place for the results of the observation, as one particular sentence in *Understanding Human Nature* reveals. "The tendency to push into the limelight, to compel the attention of parents, makes itself felt in the first days of life. Here are found the first indications of the awakening desire for recognition developing itself under the concomitant influence of the sense of inferiority, with its purpose the attainment of a goal in which the individual is seemingly superior to his environment."[84] Beginning with the observation of this demand for recognition, for acknowledgement, for "renown," Adler encloses this idea within the poorly fitting mold of the drive for power.

Adler's observations are correct, but they need to be put into other language. What he saw in the child's condition is not his inferiority but rather his basic *incompleteness*. From the beginning, the child needs others not only to survive but also to exist. He needs their warmth, their odor, their taste, their voice and their gaze, and, more and more, their words. It is not a question of a way chosen by an already autonomous subject because he realizes he is not achieving his aims all alone! This original incompleteness can never be entirely filled. In growing up, the child will learn to offer himself the assurance of his existence, but that ability does not mean that the adult, even if he knows how to live long periods without the attention of others, will be able to do completely without their recognition.

More faithful to Freud than he realizes, Adler also participates in the La Rochefoucauld tradition—the human being is selfish and solitary, but he must be encouraged to become social and generous. Others have (knowingly or not) chosen to prolong the tradition of Helvetius in setting aside any moral consideration. It is not by chance that we find such developments in several chapters of *Eroticism* of Georges Bataille, devoted to the thought of Sade. As interpreted by Blanchot (abundantly quoted here) and Bataille himself, Sade would push the idea of human isolation further than anyone at any previous time. According to Blanchot, everything in his work is founded "on absolute solitude as a first given fact. De Sade said over and over again in different ways that we are born alone, there are no links between one man and another"[85] (the Blanchot excerpts come from *Lautreamont et Sade*). "The true man knows himself to be alone and accepts the fact."[86] Bataille agrees: "The solitary man for whom he speaks pays not the slightest heed to his fellows."[87] And we must be grateful to Sade because he has given us "a true picture of a man for whom other people did not count at all."[88]

However, we know that in his own life Sade was far from indifferent to relationships that connected him with others, and Bataille delights in pointing out this paradox: an author taking it upon himself to demonstrate to others (his readers) the unimportance of these very others! He also suggests that since the solitude (prison) was being forced on him, Sade tried to make the bondage appear a free choice. On the other hand, Bataille knows perfectly well that sociality is congenital in man and "the actual make-up of every real man, inconceivable if shorn of the links made by others with him and by him with others. The independence of one man has never ceased to be any more than a boundary to the interdependence of mankind, without which there would be no human life."[89] However, Bataille thinks also that Sade's contribution to the knowledge of man is of capital importance, that the portrait of man one finds in Sade's work is true as a whole, and thus Sade has made a decisive discovery. How could this discovery be possible if Sade had really put in parentheses, for the sake of his demonstration, the basic characteristic of man?

The explanation of this new paradox lies in the fact that Bataille's thinking is dualistic, for, according to him, man himself is double. "Human life, therefore, is composed of two heterogeneous parts which never blend. One part is purposeful, given significance by utilitarian and therefore secondary ends; this part is the one we are aware of. The other is primary and sovereign, . . . either way it evades the grasp of our aware intelligence."[90] On the one hand, there is ordinary existence of normal people made up of work, care for children, kindness and loyalty, reason, conscience, language, order, usefulness, civilization, but also our fears and cowardliness. On the other hand, there is what is pathological (but part of the definition of mankind), moments of excess, the need to kill and torture without pity, barbarity, the rashness, laughter, silence—but also the passions, sensual pleasure, eroticism. Sade had the merit of giving voice to the part that is usually silent—violence—and for this reason we need to listen attentively. Our social life represses violence, but it is within us. For once we can observe it openly (in Sade); let us not close our eyes to it.

A term that characterizes the extreme of violence in man is especially important—that of sovereignty. The kings of ancient peoples were sovereigns in the sense that there was no possible limit to their power. But only literature can imagine a truly absolute sovereignty (in life one must always make compromises), and the pioneer in this aspect of literature is Sade. The blossoming of sovereignty in a subject implies the destruction of all the other subjects; they disappear or they are reduced to slavery, which, as another's tool or instrument, destroys their will. For the sovereign being, other men are divided into two categories: libertines who are similar to him and the subjugated victims. Any recognition of these victims by him would limit his sovereignty. "The man who admits the value of other people necessarily imposes limits upon himself. . . . Solidarity with everybody else prevents a man from having the sovereign attitude."[91] Here the lessons of Sade agree with those of Hegel.

We can be grateful to Sade and to his disciples and his modern interpreters, Blanchot and Bataille, for having recognized the violence in man rather than hypocritically closing their eyes to it. Still, we can wonder if Sade's originality is as radical as claimed. Moreover, we learn nothing about the place violence occupies and the role it plays in the human psyche. Is it one of the psyche's two poles, taking over the entire unconscious, passions, and eroticism, or is it only one way among many to arrive at a goal also shared by our conscious and apparently reasonable activities, our relationships with work and family?

In spite of his own warnings, Bataille views human independence as something other than a simple limit to interdependence. For him as well as for Blanchot, there exists a basic human being who has no need of others. If others intervene, we must look for the reason. It is the cowardice and weakness of sheep, say Blanchot and Bataille when they tend toward Nietzsche (Blanchot: "He [the true man] denies every element in his own nature, inherited from seventeen centuries of cowardice, that is concerned with others than himself;"[92] Bataille: "He is alone and never subject to the bounds that a common feeling of weakness imposes on other people"[93]: these attachments come only from common weakness). We seek others out of solidarity with and a respect for them, says Bataille when he wants to be on the side of common sense (humanism), as if generous feelings exhausted all forms of social interdependence. In both cases, however, the human being—even man at his finest, the human in its purest sense—ignores the social. The interhuman needs to be explained; it only surges forward as a reaction to some difficulty.

If we refuse to define sovereignty tautologically by the negation of others, it could be interpreted as an enjoyment of power. But can one enjoy power all alone? If I deny all value to others, dominating them brings me no pleasure. Thus denying others completely annuls, rather than reinforces, sovereignty. That paradox is one Hegel took pleasure in exploring. Bataille reaches the same conclusion but by a more tortuous route. The movement of destruction that enlivens the subject, he suggests, ends up striking him; the extreme sadist would not be able to escape his own blows and finds he has become a masochist. "If we start from the principle of denying others posited by de Sade it is strange to observe that at the very peak of unlimited denial of others is a denial of oneself."[94] This negation of self is not strange at all, however, and it appears well before reaching the extreme of denying others. The two begin simultaneously, for one does not exist without the other. The absolute tyrant is absolutely unhappy. The path of the master, said Hegel, leads to an impasse. The cases of a truly solitary pleasure—those in which I would need no gaze or recognition from another to enjoy my capacity to reduce with impunity other beings to nothing—are almost impossible, and they do not reveal the truth of the human condition. Solitude is only a special case of social interaction, not its opposite. The opposite of sociability simply does not exist.

Among the different descriptions of human dualism that Bataille proposes, he also uses an economic model. "Erotic conduct is the opposite of normal conduct as spending is the opposite of getting. If we follow the dictates of reason we try to acquire all kinds of goods . . . we use all means to get richer and to possess more. . . . But when the fever of sex seizes us we behave in the opposite way. We recklessly draw on our strength."[95] This idea of fortuitous spending is the basis for Bataille's "general economy," described in *The Accursed Share*. With new costs, the author shows us the classic opposition between personal interest and the passions that Adam Smith went far beyond (for Smith, says Dupuy, "morality and economy are the subject of one and the same science").[96] But can we accumulate the benefits of human exchange in the same way as riches? Can love or friendship or the interaction in the workplace be described as an attempt to receive without giving? Conversely, do we *receive* nothing in an erotic passion? If I make another live intensely, for this I get greater gratification: Human exchange cannot be divided up according to the usual columns in account books. When Jesus told his disciples, "Lend without any hope of return. You will have a great reward,"[97] he showed himself a better psychologist than Bataille.

Bataille's anthropology remains inside the tradition of asocial psychology while absorbing several elements of the Hegelian version. Essential man is solitary; he only joins his fellowmen out of weakness and lack of courage. Society is on the side of civilization and morality; the unconscious is silent and violent. In reintroducing these traditional dichotomies, Bataille leaves us an equally unsatisfactory picture of sociality and the unconscious. Sociality is in no way secondary or an afterthought, and the demand for recognition through the gaze of another is neither moral (generosity) nor immoral (vanity); it is necessarily present. The unconscious is never independent of others, of those who surround us from the beginning. Violence is not opposed to the useful, for even violence has a purpose.

The positions represented by traditional psychology or by authors like Bataille remain very popular today. Does this enduring popularity mean that the asocial theories rule uncontested over the field of general psychology? Without even mentioning the great European novelists, who, as René Girard has reminded us, have always shown man as dependent on other men (the "mimetic desire" of Girard is only another name for the *amour-propre* of Rousseau), we can observe that, as in the past, currents exist in philosophy as well as psychoanalysis that assume the basic sociality of man. Ludwig Feuerbach in *Principles of the Philosophy of the Future* (1842) makes communication between men and the human community the very definition of humanity. It is also the meaning Feuerbach gives the well-known affirmation according to which the difference between men and animals lies in the presence or absence of a conscience, the representation of existence within the mind. Whoever says conscience, says intersubjectivity, community, communication. For Feuerbach as well as for Rousseau, the very sentiment of existence, the foundation of conscience, comes from life lived in society. In the twentieth century the elaboration of a new philosophical anthropology will make its way, often on the margins of philosophy, as an intersubjective anthropology (sometimes expressed in extremely abstract terms) in authors as different as Martin Buber and Mikhail Bakhtin, Emmanuel Lévinas and Jürgen Habermas.

In psychoanalysis the asocial model of man underlying the Freudian vulgate has also been questioned for some time. There are two subtraditions that must be distinguished. One, which we can trace back to Ferenczi, questions the "paternal" orientation of Freud and insists on the relations between mother and infant established in the "preoedipal" phase, rejoining here the speculations of Bachofen on the "maternal right" and uncovering non-conflicting relations at the beginning of individual life. No matter how profoundly we delve into the human spirit, claims Ferenczi, we never find an isolated being but only relationship with others. The most significant representatives of this tendency are two Hungarians who form a link with the "British School": Alice Balint, who studies "primary love" (between mother and child), and Michael Balint, whose concept of the "basic default" describes the origin of "preoedipal" mental disturbances.

Some British psychoanalysts, in particular Melanie Klein and W. R. D. Fairbairn, call themselves specialists of "object relations," but if we remember that the "object" in question is another subject (*alter* facing *ego*), it would be more accurate to speak of their ideas as an *intersubjective psychoanalysis*. Michael Balint vigorously criticizes the Freudian idea of a primary narcissism as an original autoeroticism and therefore an initial self-sufficiency of the individual. He shows that the relationship to the parent (the mother) is immediately present and that it does not characterize only weak individuals. Among the "object relations," certain ones are more important in the eyes of this school. With Balint or Fairbairn, it is no longer the "Oedipus complex," a tangle of rivalry and conflict, that constitutes the rock on which the human psyche is built but a much earlier relationship that links the newborn and his parent, a relationship of attachment and dependence (the "primary love" of Alice Balint).

The other subtradition starts from Marxist critiques of Freudianism in Erich Fromm, or from the social, culturalist, and feminist criticism of Karen Horney, and finally from the interpersonal psychiatry of Harry Stack Sullivan in the United States. (In the thirties, Fromm and Horney, fleeing Germany's Nazism, as Bettelheim did several years later, rejoined Sullivan there.) They were later joined by certain "ego" psychologists and established close collaboration with anthropologists. The representatives of this psychoanalytic current have deplored the absence in Freud of interest in social interaction and have tried to combine the psychoanalytic findings with a study of social forms in different contemporary political regimes, totalitarianism and democracy.

Fromm has also called attention to another aspect of the Freudian model, the reference to the economic model to describe psychic life. It is not a question of just any model, but of the one in current use in the nineteenth century, one that implies the fundamental solitude and autarchy of man. "The individual, primarily alone and self-sufficient, enters into economic relations with others as means to one end: to sell and to buy. Freud's concept of human relations is essentially the same: the individual appears fully equipped with biologically given drives, which need to be satisfied. In order to satisfy them, the individual enters into relations with other 'objects.' Other individuals thus are always a means to one's end, the satisfaction of strivings which in themselves originate in the individual before he enters into contact with others. The field of human relations in Freud's sense is similar to the market—it is an exchange of satisfaction of biologically given needs."[98] It is useless to insist on the fact that such a picture of human exchange is profoundly unsatisfying. It is a distortion in two senses. For one, this economic model does not allow for an understanding of economic reality itself. For another, it forces us to make relationships between persons identical with our relationship to things. In the present case no goods are transmitted independently of subjects put in contact with each other, and the gift of love is not like other spending. Here, the more one gives, the more one possesses. Even if numerous developments in Freud's theory escape this general frame (for example, we could not explain the action of the superego by any random "pleasure principle" nor conceive of it outside relationships with others), it nevertheless is true that it rests fundamentally on a not very believable psychological hedonism.

Few arguments of the original Freudian theory have escaped being justifiably criticized, but Freud's prestige is still felt today and rightly so. A work like his is not made up only of propositions describing the human psyche; it is also impregnated with Freud's extraordinary personality and with the intensity of his personal engagement (altogether different from a selfish narcissism) and the force of his writing. The reverse side of this well-deserved admiration, however, is the reticence of theoreticians who came after Freud to openly oppose him. It is clear that the transformation of the Freudian legacy into a sacred and dogmatic text is contrary to one of the inspirations that gave life to Freud's enterprise. In principle he put the search for truth above the respect for authority and hoped, at least throughout part of his life, that his hypotheses would eventually be surpassed and abandoned. But far from joining together to slay and devour the father, in accord with his theory, these authors, often themselves analyzed by the founder's own analysands, all claim to remain faithful to Freud even when they question the basic postulates of his system. This position is true of authors as different as Fromm or Lacan, Balint or Winnicott.

Nevertheless, we need to point out that, thanks to their efforts, a new psychoanalysis—no longer drive-based and therefore individual as Freud's, but rather relational—has been in place, incognito, for fifty years. When Fairbairn stated, in his now famous formula: "Libido is primarily object-seeking (rather than pleasure-seeking, as in the classic theory),"[99] he brought about a true revolution. The "object," that is, the other subject, becomes the aim of human activity (which no longer needs to always be called the "libido"). Unfortunately, none of these innovative psychoanalysts have had the vigorousness of thought or the commitment to writing necessary to create a work comparable to Freud's.

Differences exist between the representatives of these diverse branches of contemporary psychoanalysis, but their contributions are complementary rather than contradictory. For example, the American "culturalist" school insisted on the need for recognition and a struggle for prestige, while the English school of "object relations" spotlighted the need for comfort and attachment felt by the infant or the process of "introjection" of good and bad "objects." The same can be said of other contributions to the knowledge of human sociality, coming from sociology, ethnology, or, in a particularly suggestive domain, the psychology of development, which no longer studies only the process of cognitive acquisition but also analyzes the "affective," thus relational, evolution of the child. The necessary bridges between the schools, and even more between the disciplines, are, however, slow and difficult to construct (the work of the Briton, John Bowlby, may be the beginning of such a synthesis).

Before we enter into the heart of the matter, another question remains to be asked. In order to examine the great philosophical and psychological traditions and the picture of man they conceal, we find we are obliged to look for an explanation of their blindness in the face of such obvious facts and of the tacit or open acceptance of such an improbable conception. Why has the account of the individual's origin, which can be observed by everyone in the development of the child, been replaced by an account of the origin of the species, which must necessarily be mythical and the product of ideology alone? Why imagine a solitary being to whom we have never had and never will have access? Why consider only the relations of rivalry, thus similarity, between men and ignore those of contiguity and complementarity? Why reduce all sociality to morality and all amorality to solitude? The response to these questions is certainly not to be looked for in the intellectual weakness of our authors. But where, then? Even if I do not know how to give a final answer, I am sure these questions are worth asking. Here are several reflections they elicit in me.

If the account of the origin of the species has been systematically preferred over that of the origin of the individual, the phylogenesis to the ontogenesis, it is without doubt in part due to the fact that the authors of these accounts are men, not women, and always ready to receive as an audacious revelation, as a cleansing truth, the claims for an evil and thus selfish, solitary human nature. Those who resist this simplification are immediately accused of being moralistic and cowardly: They do not dare face the truth.

Another specifically modern reason for this repression may be the confusion of mental categories with those that are no longer moral but political. Our attachment to equality as a political ideal makes us project this model onto social reality itself. As a result, when we admit that it is impossible to avoid social relations, we reduce them to those that presuppose equality: rivalry, imitation. Unconsciously, we see society in the image of democracy as described by its earliest critics—an endless battle between rivals that are not organized into hierarchies. What Bonald thinks about democracies (that they favor unlimited competition), Nietzsche attributes to all men. But any society, even a democratic one, includes as many, if not more, unegalitarian (hierarchical) relationships as egalitarian. How can we otherwise understand the connection between parent and child, student and teacher, employee and employer, artist and public? It is perhaps this same omnipresence of the egalitarian idea in our society that explains our attraction to the economic model as a way to represent human interaction; converting everything into a commodity allows us to eliminate (or to ignore) the hierarchical differences between persons.

A final cause for our blindness might be found on the side of vanity, in this case that of the thinker, scholar, or philosopher. Perhaps it is unflattering for the human species to describe itself as wicked, but it is flattering for the individual to think of himself as owing nothing to anyone and carrying on a solitary search for truth rather than for the approval of his public. It is out of pride that men profess different variants of the asocial idea, that they heap so many sins and crimes on themselves, so much selfishness, brutality, parricide! It is in painting themselves as wicked that they declare themselves alone. The benefit they draw from this inference makes up generously for the drawbacks resulting from their declaration.

In heaping these crimes on themselves, they can hide their basic incompleteness and present themselves as masters of their destiny. They are ready to admit anything but their dependence, their need of others. They arrive at their goal by considering relationships with others as purely optional. Thus the contents of the theory guarantee the value of the one who presents it.

2 To Be, to Live, to Exist

It is difficult in our times to discuss the mental structure of a human being without referring to the Freudian conception. This thought, so unorthodox when it first appeared, has become our orthodoxy; Freudian terminology has become part of current usage, and we are obliged to begin with it. However, the general terms of the theory proposed by Freud have, as we all know, undergone important changes between the first formulations and their final syntheses. In the beginning Freud identifies two large groups of drives that dominate our activities: those of self-preservation (directed toward myself) and the sexual urges (directed toward others). In this respect, as Freud himself does not fail to point out, he is continuing what is already a long tradition: A line of Schiller's claims that love and hunger drive the world (hunger in Freud is the most important example of self-preservation), and Kant also reduced our instincts to two, "*love of life and sexual love*, . . . Love of life aims at the preservation of the individual; sexual love, at that of the species."[1]

Several clinical observations and profound reflection, however, would lead Freud not to precisely reject this traditional distinction but rather to limit its extent and to include it as a simple subdivision in another structuring, which would now become dominant. In one way, the study of narcissism would persuade Freud that self-preservation could be included in self-love, and there would no longer be a clear contrast between these two variants of love even though this term (or that of "Eros" or "libido") is given greater extension. This merging must in itself bother Freud, who called himself a "dualist" and who always thought in binary oppositions. But the duality will be found again at another level. All the "erotic" drives, or life urges, now array themselves against the death wish, sometimes called "the nirvana principle" (in his youthful writings Freud also uses the expression "inertia principle").

Surely structural reasons (the necessity of proceeding by oppositions) are not the only ones that encouraged Freud (in *Beyond the Pleasure Principle*) to introduce the idea of the death wish. For this principle too, there were positive and substantial reasons of basically two kinds. First, Freud observed certain phenomena of repetition, including some profoundly disagreeable situations that could not be explained by any search for pleasure and therefore by life drives. Second, he was led to admit that aggressive and destructive behavior, whether directed against the ego itself or against the outside world and therefore others, cannot always be explained in sexual terms. Freud comes to believe that sexual perversions—and here the labels masochism and sadism come immediately to mind—are only secondary formations, combinations of sexual drives and death urges. Behind them is a kind of innate (nonsexual) masochism and innate aggressivity, a destruction of the self and of the other. "And now the instincts that we believe in divide themselves into two groups—the erotic instincts, which seek to combine more and more living substance into ever greater unities, and the death instincts, which oppose this effort and lead what is living back into an inorganic state. From the concurrent and opposing action of these two proceed the phenomena of life which are brought to an end by death."[2]

However, one wonders if the two positive sources put forth in this new idea, the tendency toward repetition and aggressivity, can be applied to the same process. With Freud himself, we see a wavering in the use of terminology, which is pointed out by

Laplanche and Pontalis in the *Language of Psychoanalysis*. In his interpretation of repetition, Freud wavers between the progressive reduction of a substance to nothing (bringing it closer to aggressivity) and its preservation in the earlier state, which would make it easier to distinguish. "The definitions which Freud proposes," Laplanche and Pontalis point out, "are all ambiguous in that the tendency towards an absolute reduction and the trend to constancy are treated as identical."[3] Here Freud is led to speak of "destruction" and "conservation" as if they were synonyms. He wavers between several sets of terms. The inertia principle and that of nirvana both lead toward reduction; on the other hand, the principle of constancy (probably an echo of the "stability principle" introduced by Fechner) and homeostasis, with all the allusions to the second principle of thermodynamics, go back to the idea of stability, of immobile equilibrium, from repetition to the identical.

We never actually abandon Freudian thought in keeping these two ingredients separated rather than merging them. Deep in each person there must be an urge to remain identical to himself and immobile, to infinitely repeat what already exists. And why speak only of the human being? Is not this same tendency at work in every being and even in all matter? It is to this quality of matter that Spinoza seems to refer in his famous proposition: "Everything in so far as it is in itself endeavours to persist in its own being."[4] This effort, this propensity for being, however, is not life. It is not death either—the passing from organic to inorganic as Freud suggests. However, it has an unhealthy character, since it consolidates in the living being that which is part of inert matter. It is not a transformation of one into other but rather the manifestation of the inorganic element in the organic, an expression of matter itself. To be taken over by this transformation to the inorganic (which every human recognizes as a mental state), by this fascination with nothingness, is certainly an unhealthy behavior, but it does not in itself imply active destruction or aggressivity.

Let us look now at aggressivity. We may first say that the aggressive act can be described by the position of the object of the aggression and the person who commits it. The situation most frequently mentioned suggests a certain similarity between the aggressor and his target; we are rivals in trying to obtain the same object or the same favor, and I attack the other to occupy (alone) this coveted place. Thus aggression is only a way to obtain recognition; it is the elimination of rivals. In the case of Bataille, we glimpsed another kind of aggression aimed at those we judge inferior. The search for recognition is not absent here either, even though it takes a paradoxical form, since submission and even the physical destruction of the person become the way I prove my sovereignty to myself or to a third party (the kind of pleasure felt by a torturer or a murderer). A third form of aggression is even more directly linked to the search for recognition, that which I direct toward its potential holders, my superiors, in order to avenge myself on them for refusing me recognition. It is the aggression of the dismissed lover, of the child who attacks his negligent parents, the bad student who attacks his teacher, the indigent who curses a disappointing benefactor.

A fourth kind of aggression, auto-aggression, can appear different at first glance. Can this type of aggression be considered an indirect way of looking for recognition? Doesn't an innate, irreducible masochism exist? The question is worth a closer look, but we can already see that, from the child's act of deliberately hurting himself to attract the attention of his parents to that of the person who commits suicide and leaves behind a message for those who failed to love him, these self-destructive acts are frequently also the result of interaction with others and a demand for recognition. It is certainly reasonable that aggressiveness or the drive to destroy are not separate drives but one way among others taken by our psyche in its search for satisfactions, the same search in which we are engaged the rest of the time.

We could wonder too if there is not a certain admission of impotence in trying to explain our behavior by arbitrarily postulating an "urge" or an "instinct" as the origin, as a sufficient cause. To say that an "urge of aggression" explains our aggressiveness is like explaining our propensity for sleep by a "sleep instinct." Here I pick up the conclusions of Fromm but limit them to the drive to aggression and exclude the urge to repetition. In fact, with regard to the urges to live and to die, Fromm writes, "This duality, however, is not one of two biologically inherent instincts, relatively constant and always battling with each other until the final victory of the death instinct, but it is one between the primary and most fundamental tendency of life . . . and its contradiction, which comes into being when man fails in this goal. In this view the 'death instinct' . . . represents *psychopathology* and not, as in Freud's view, a part of *normal biology*."[5]

The drives of aggression and hate are not qualitatively different from what Freud calls the life drives, sexual and self-preservation, "love" and "hunger." But we can now ask, from the standpoint of recognition, do these expressions conceal homogeneous realities? There is certainly in us an instinct for preservation of the species and reproduction, and it can be satisfied without obtaining the attention of another, as can a part of physical pleasure itself, a phenomenon we can observe just as well in the sex life of a dog. Obviously, however, we cannot reduce to this kind of satisfaction the immense field of love and eroticism in which the existence of another plays a basic role. On the other hand, no doubt hunger and thirst drive us to eat and to drink, but this fact is a very incomplete explanation of the contents of our plates, bowls, or glasses. We eat this or that according to our ethnic, social, and family traditions, according to the social value of different foods and taking into account the people in whose company we find ourselves.

In other words, there are two levels of organization in our "life urges": one that we share with all living organisms—the urge to satisfy hunger and thirst and the urge to seek agreeable sensations—and the other, specifically human, based on our original incompleteness and on our social nature—relationships between individuals. Victor Hugo said [in *William Shakespeare*]: "Animals live, man exists," and we could in these terms call the first level of organization that of "living," the second, that of "existing."

In starting with the Freudian distinction between life and death drives, we end up with a three part division—between being, living, and existing. The urge to be we share with all matter, the urge to live with all living creatures, but the urge to exist is specifically human.

THE THREE STAGES

What is human should not be reduced to what is specifically human. Man is first a material object, and this property dictates certain types of behavior. He is at the same time a living being, an animal, and he shares characteristics with animals. A second group of behavior patterns can be explained by this fact. But he is also a human being unlike any other living being, who exists in society, in the company of other men. These three levels, cosmic, animal, and social, are irreducible to each other even if certain borderline cases can always be found.

The first frontier, therefore, lies between being and living, between stability and change, between identity with oneself and transformation. Extreme behavior caused by the drive to live are prostration, serious depression, the loss of self in nothingness, but actions that are partially influenced by this drive are much more common. Who does not remember those moments when we feel as though we have become wood or stone or cement, when our entire being seems to become inanimate, when nothing interests us any longer, when we no longer want to talk or even to move except according to old habits, when others no longer exist, when we take nourishment rather than eat, when perception dies, when we are victims of an unyielding torpor? This immobility certainly does not enrich us, but enrichment is not what we ask of it. It has a reassuring effect on us even though its action is really negative. Paradoxically, it is our unique immediate experience of the infinite and the absolute. It consists only of nothingness; the always temporary constructions of life are necessarily finite, partial, relative.

A more active version of this state consists in making obsessive and mechanical gestures, continuing with actions that make no sense but that have been used in the past. Attitudes that, on certain days, seem to cover the totality of existence: clipping the hedge in the yard, cleaning the house or the car, straightening up, that is, reestablishing an order we hope will never change, going over the elements of a collection. This repeating of the same thing is equally contrary to life. "It is the recurrence of the same sensual impressions which chiefly keeps men in check and confines them to a narrow field,"[6] remarks Karl Philipp Moritz, a subtle observer of human behavior, in his fictionalized autobiography, *Anton Reiser*.

Finally, it is necessary to consider a more positive drive to life, an identification with the world around us, a dissolving into the cosmos, which allows us to feel like growing grass or a pebble shining in the sun. Rousseau tells us about this kind of experience in the famous fifth *Reverie*, a state of immobility and repetition that allows us to forget our constitutive incompleteness (a state that, in fact, neither the animals nor the plants have): "a state in which the soul finds a solid enough base to rest itself on entirely and to gather its whole being into without needing to recall the past or encroach upon the future; in which time is nothing for it; in which the present lasts forever without, however, making its duration noticed and without any trace of time's passage; without any sentiment of deprivation or of enjoyment, pleasure or pain, desire or fear, except that of our existence, and having this sentiment alone fill it completely."[7] Having emptied oneself of one's humanity, one attains "a sufficient, perfect, and full happiness which leaves the soul no emptiness it might feel a need to fill."[8]

It is clear, however, that this sensation, which corresponds to an absence of humanity, does not exactly cover what Rousseau himself elsewhere called the feeling of existence. What we have here is more a feeling of being. This attitude resembles states as diverse as Buddhist deliverance, Stoic detachment, or Christian quietism (all of which also imply an acceptance of the world as it is, a renunciation of the temptation to make it conform to our wishes). If I blend harmoniously with the universe, I do not need to save a special place for my essential needs or for human coexistence. Here we find, in the place of social incompleteness, a cosmic fulfillment. My feeling of being is on a level with that of a butterfly, of the flower, or of the waves of the sea.

The second important frontier separates living and existing. It is denied by numerous schools of thought that might be called biological. Schopenhauer, an important source of inspiration for Freud, has been one of their important spokesmen. For example, he writes: "The foundation of our whole nature, and, therefore, of our happiness, is our physique, and the most essential factor in happiness is health. . . . There can be no competition or compensation between these essential factors on the one side, and honor, pomp, rank, and reputation on the other, however much value we may set upon the latter. . . . We should add very much to our happiness by a timely recognition of the simple truth that every man's chief and real existence is in his own skin and not in other people's opinions."[9] In like fashion, for Schopenhauer the psychology of love is reduced to the need to reproduce the species. Here is a very debatable point. Man *lives* perhaps first of all in his skin, but he does not begin to *exist* except through the gaze of others, and without existence life itself dies out. Each of us is born twice, in nature and in society, to life and to existence. Both life and existence are fragile, but the dangers threatening them are not the same. Certainly, man is an animal, but that is not all he is.

From a biological perspective also (which sees in the biological not only the basis for all human life but also its purpose), one can find the presence of interhuman relationships from the youngest age, but here they are considered instrumental, established in view of something other than themselves: the infant certainly needs its mother, but it is in order to eat. This same mentality later tries to explain human behavior by a so-called pleasure principle. But this hedonistic concept does not explain our psychological choices in adult life any better than it explains our economic decisions. The great contribution of Fairbairn is to have declared that desire does not search for pleasure but rather for relations. Relations with others are not a means (to fill the stomach or for sexual gratification); they are the goal we search for to reassure us of our existence (pleasure itself can become a way to establish a relationship). Fairbairn made his discovery while observing abused children who were ill treated, beaten, tortured by their parents but who, nevertheless, never wanted to leave home. How can this phenomenon be explained? By postulating a "suffering drive"? Certainly not. It is rather that they prefer the blows coming from their parents to the caresses offered by strangers. The blows were a (painful) form of recognition, but the caresses of strangers did nothing to reinforce their feeling of existence.

The assimilation of "social" needs into biological ones such as hunger, which is a common practice today, is very misleading. It describes the relationship between people as though it were a relationship to things. I can appropriate a thing—it was far away at first, now it is close to me. If I eat an apple, it ceases to exist; I transform it permanently into a food assimilated by my body. But nothing comparable can come from my relations with a person (at least, if he or she is not changed into an object, a practice for which, sadly, there are numerous examples, but then the person cannot confirm my existence). Enjoying this person does not imply his destruction. By interiorizing him, I do not diminish his autonomy. The thing exchanged here cannot be separated from the very process of exchange, as an object that is passed from hand to hand could be. What I desire is the relationship itself—love, comfort, recognition—not something this relationship can get for me. I can never be filled with pleasures (or recognition) in the way one pours liquid into a goatskin.

The satisfaction of the urge to live and the urge to exist can be fulfilled at the same time, in which case we have trouble distinguishing them. The satisfaction of one can also work against that of the other, however, and it is not certain, as Schopenhauer seems to think, that we would rather live than exist. We frequently renounce sensual pleasures, food and sexual fulfillment, in a search for "symbolic" pleasures, the approval of others or of a part of our own conscience. We can go even further and deliberately choose physical discomfort in order to obtain what we believe to be a moral purification. We fast, we practice abstinence, we become a monk or flagellate ourselves to mortify the flesh. As a general rule, these situations are less obvious. Moritz describes the behavior of his hero in this way: "Although Reiser took real pleasure in the book he was reading, the pleasure of being seen in that position by the Precentor was far greater. This shows his tendency to vanity: he cared more for the appearance than the thing itself, although he did not regard this either as unimportant."[10]

The frontier separating living and existing is the one that also distinguishes man from the animals. Of course, the real line is not as airtight as the isolated words would lead us to believe. Not only does man live, just as animals do, but the animals exist, just as man does, even if it is to a lesser degree. The little monkey, just as the child, needs to be protected, reassured, and comforted. In paying court, monkeys "make eyes at each other." The eye-to-eye gaze for many animals means a threat, and it often suffices to get a young troublemaker back into line for the leader of the pack to look him in the eye. Domestic animals intentionally seek human recognition. There are as many examples of social coexistence communicated here, as they are with men, by a look. Nevertheless, these moments of coexistence that remind us of human characteristics are limited in time and have a restricted role. Life takes over from existence most of the time, while the opposite is true for man. The human conscience does not suddenly appear out of nowhere; it is prepared by the forms of animal life, but yet it is impossible to confuse the embryonic state with a developed one.

The need to exist can never be completely satisfied; no coexistence already lived delivers us from the demand for new coexistences. The reason for this basic incompleteness is not the inevitable socialization of a desiring being who is fundamentally solitary, but rather the disparity between an endless demand and its satisfaction, which is always partial and temporary. This need is born soon after our physical birth and does not cease until the unconsciousness that precedes death. The recognition of our existence, which is the preliminary condition for all existence, is the soul's oxygen. The fact that I breathe today does not dispense with the need for air tomorrow, and past recognitions will not be sufficient for me in the present. It is only out of naiveté or ill will that we try to console those who deplore the absence of acknowledgment today by reminding them of yesterday's successes. Instead, this reminder makes the lack of it now even more painful. The laurels of last year emphasize more than they compensate for the absence of laurels freshly cut. I can lower my demands, create for myself a system of secondary compensations (or even tertiary compensations!), but whatever the number of recognitions already received, I cannot finally do without new ones.

The comparison between the need for recognition and the need to breathe is not completely fortuitous, and we find it in the writings of very different authors. Moritz uses it in describing the image of self with which each one is endowed: "The self confidence which is as necessary for moral activity as breathing is for bodily movement,"[11] but self confidence is essentially a positive image which others might have of me and that I have internalized. Others are like the air for me, says Balint, on the outside as well as the inside, in the atmosphere and in my lungs, and just as imperceptible. I only discover how necessary it is to me when I risk not having it. To be deprived of coexistence is to suffocate. In the absence of any recognition, dread and fear rush in, which, like angina, causes physical symptoms of suffocation, of asphyxiation. It takes us by the throat. When we are oppressed, the lungs seem to no longer want to dilate.

The physical condition of the lack of recognition is solitude. If others are absent, by definition we cannot capture their gaze. But what is even more painful than physical solitude, which can be improved or enlivened in different ways, is to live among others without receiving any sign from them. William James formulated this situation well in his description of the "Social Self": "A man's Social Self is the recognition which he gets from his mates. We are not only gregarious animals, liking to be in sight of our fellows, but we have an innate propensity to get ourselves noticed, and noticed favorably, by our kind. No more fiendish punishment could be devised, were such a thing physically possible, than that one should be turned loose in society and remain absolutely unnoticed by all the members thereof."[12] It is the position of the outsider, the stranger, the excluded, that makes us recognize this. The poor, Adam Smith has already suggested, are those no one notices, who never manage to exist in the eyes of their fellow citizens. "The poor man goes out and comes in unheeded, and when in the midst of a crowd is in the same obscurity as if shut up in his own hovel."[13] The "invisible man" is also the American black in the classic description of Ralph Ellison. "I am invisible, understand, simply because people refuse to see me. . . . you often doubt if you really exist . . . You ache with the need to convince yourself that you do exist in the real world . . . you curse and you swear to make them recognize you."[14]

Old age is also a reduction, not only of vital forces but also of existence. The principle cause is increased solitude. "I began my death with solitude," wrote Victor Hugo. Existence can die even before life is snuffed out. The social being in an old person is progressively "disconnected" from the different lines that connected him; boredom becomes the main characteristic of his life.

Habitual sources of recognition disappear, one after the other (natural selection); and those who replace him—the "new generations"—no longer feel any interest in him nor he in them (voluntary selection). They have no need of the old nor do the old of them, even when the drive to exist remains.

There is a "solitude of the dying," that is, of the old person, which is specifically modern, says Norbert Elias. We fear death and anything that makes us think about it, and we prefer to put out of sight anything that reminds us of it. Old people are put in retirement homes where they see only other old people, and we thus rid ourselves of this unseemly sight, but they receive only a tiny feeling of existence in these places, where they are not with those who were important in their lives but with unknown people who, in addition, are like them and therefore useless. A plurality of solitary people does not create a society. The next step is the hospital, where, in our time, the majority of old people die. We care for their organs, not their being, and we try to prolong their life but not their existence. Old people die alone; existence has left them before life itself.

THE ORIGIN OF INDIVIDUALS

The origin of the species is unknown to us; that of individuals is evident every day in the development of our children. I would now like to take up this origin in offering an "ideal" story, based on the observations of contemporary psychologists but simplified and made more general. How does existence emerge? What are the elementary social interactions, irreducible one to the other, on which the complex interactions of the adult world are built? There is no unanimous response to these questions. The psychologists and psychoanalysts of childhood have often been so impressed by a particular finding they make that they want to apply it to all childhood activities. If everything is not aggression, they tell us, then it is love or attachment or comfort or care, each of these terms describing the whole of parent-child relationships. We can wonder if, rather than concurrent interpretations of the same fact, we are not faced with different facts that we must try to arrange in relation to each other. The task is not always easy.

It is made especially arduous by the truly singular character of this being, the newborn, which we try, of course, to assimilate into more familiar realities. Psychologists do not escape this temptation. Some speak, even after birth, of a total symbiosis between mother and child. However, this symbiosis can exist only metaphorically and only in the mind of the mother, never in that of the child. Others, capitulating no doubt to an unconscious adultocentrism, project into babyhood a much later state of mind. It is only from the viewpoint of a fully developed man that we can see the child of the man as the incarnation of an initial selfishness (Piaget) or an infantile autism (Mahler), or describe his evolution as an effort to overcome his powerlessness (Fairbairn) or to attain independence (Winnicott). In reality, it is not easy to think of this initial stage as one in which the two beings, child and parent, are well separated and where one, however, has such need of the other.

One thing is clear, however, whatever terms we use to describe it: The child is born with a need for others and with a predisposition to establish contact with them. To speak as Rousseau, "It is man's weakness which makes him sociable."[15] From the first hours of his life, he recognizes one object among all the others: the human face, which he identifies by the presence of eyes. In the first weeks of life, he also distinguishes the human voice from other sounds.

As for his need of others, it certainly extends to what I am calling life. The baby could not survive without being nourished by someone other than himself. But this obvious biological dependency has too long served to conceal another dependency that is social, the need to exist and not just to live. Everything seems to indicate that the two dependencies are distinct from the outset. The need to be comforted is not a substitute for being fed. This difference has been better understood since Harlow's famous experiment on small monkeys, who preferred a dummy mother that could offer them the same contact as their real mother to a dummy that feeds them but which they cannot rub against. In the same way, and even more so, the infant needs to be carried, rocked, surrounded by affectionate sounds and contacts, not just fed. The first distance the infant focuses on is not the two centimeters to the breast he wants to suck, but the twenty centimeters to the face of his mother.

To identify the important phases of his development as oral, anal, and genital is too biological a picture of an individual's evolution. These "stages," established by Abraham and adopted by Freud, illustrate not only the sexual postulate of the theory—"normal" (adult) sexuality being the goal to attain and the body of the child divided according to the exclusive needs of the theory—but also his antisocial spirit. None of these stages is identified by a specific relationship to others, as if all that counted for the infant were already contained in his own body. The infant looks around even before he nurses, but the appropriate recognition of this "scopic" stage is still awaited (the "mirror stage" of Lacan is an ambiguous step in this direction).

Genetic psychology established long ago that the baby's development does not proceed by the acquisition of radically new elements but rather by a diversification and specialization of activities that are present from the beginning and appear to us afterwards as syncretic. The infant is predisposed toward sociability from birth, but this disposition to interaction becomes increasingly more complex and nuanced, at least until he arrives at adulthood. The affective does not precede the cognitive, the self does not come before others, all of this is present at the same time before diversifying and perfecting itself.

The most elementary distinction is between a passive principle and an active one. In the interaction, the infant wants to be both patient and agent. He is passive when he is being comforted by his parents, active when he sets out to explore his environment. He wants both to be reassured and to be stimulated, to be certain of the known and to discover the unknown. He practices, to use the language of Piaget, assimilation (of the world to him) and accommodation (of himself to the world) at the same time. This basic duality is not the same as an opposition between the need for others and the assertion of oneself. The infant asserts himself just as well by his dependence on others as by his curiosity about the outside world, and his need of others underlies both of these activities. The alternation of more or less active or passive moments finds itself reinforced by parallel alternation of presence and absence on the part of the parent, by moments of protection and comfort, on the one hand, and of abandonment, on the other. These moments of separation are no less constructive for the relation to others than are the moments of presence. The infant must feel himself reassured in order to launch into the exploration of the unknown world around him, but it is the absence that leads him to progressively construct the identity of the parent, to become conscious of the passing of time, which will prepare him for the acquisition of language. This same inevitable absence, no matter how temporary, will make him sensitive, little by little, to his original incompleteness, to the fact that he does not make up a self-sufficient whole. The rest of his life will be devoted to attempts to fill this basic default (if one can use, changing the sense a little, the expression of Balint).

The infant's diversification of social contact is continuous, but for purposes of discussion, it is better to distinguish between stages that are characterized by the acquisition of a new form of interaction. Admittedly, their separation contains some arbitrariness. The changes do not take place on only one level, different aspects of personality do not evolve at the same speed, and giving preference to one aspect over another inevitably leads to neglecting others. There are also enormous variations in the individual development of children; any indication of age can only be taken as

Stage 3: Manipulation (from 5 to 9 months). At the beginning of this period an important physical change takes place: The infant acquires greater skill in his movements and an ability to manipulate the objects around him. Everything new fascinates him, and he avidly assimilates. As a consequence, he turns somewhat from human interaction to concentrate on the world of objects. Human beings become either objects among others that he tries to explore and handle or partners in this exploration. We can say that the initial dyad finds itself replaced during this period by triadic situations made up of two subjects and an object. Now the relationships of alternating and collaborating are reinforced. The gesture of pointing, at this point not well elaborated, represents this interaction. It brings one object to the attention of another subject. The infant also learns the name of certain objects at this time. An increasing manual dexterity leads him from the exploration of objects to their manipulation; they move according to his movements.

Stage 4: Memory (from 9 to 18 months). According to numerous authors, the changes that arise around the ninth month are so important that they deserve to be considered as a second birth, a definitive entry into the world of humans. The development of the mind and of memory allows the child to internalize the temporal dimension, and because of this development, he begins to identify the individuals around him. People are completely separated from things. The infant's life now revolves around familiar individuals whom he identifies easily, and he is afraid of strangers. He also remembers the past enough for it to influence his behavior. Where, for example, the little monkey always shows signs of contentment when his mother reappears before him after an absence, the little human can easily choose to "pout," to punish the parent for his past absence. In doing so, he imitates the parent, who was able to refuse to pay him any attention. The quasi-dialogue of the preceding stages gives way now to a real dialogue (although still not verbal), and, as in the well-known and beloved game of "peek-a-boo," reciprocity is born. Finally, recognizing the other as a partner in the dialogue, the child constitutes himself as subject and discovers intentionality. He now takes an action because he wants to, not in reaction to external appeals. He also begins to perceive a clear difference between the group adult-parents and the group children-companions, between asymmetrical and symmetrical partners. Acts of rivalry between members of the same age group become possible. Triadic structures now contain three distinct subjects.

Stage 5: Language (after 18 months). The acquisition of language is prepared by the mastery of actions established during previous stages. On the one hand, the child has reinforced in himself, mainly through play, the capacity to symbolize, that is to associate two entities in a stable fashion, even if one is absent. This capacity is also a rudiment of the process of reference or designation of segments of the world. On the other hand, the child is familiar with the practice of preverbal "dialogue," of collaboration with a partner and with a common goal directing the actions of both participants. Language, the use of preestablished verbal signs, combines these two functions, referential and communicative, while enormously extending them. Now all objects can be designated along with all situations, and communication can take place with everyone who knows the same code, that is, the same language. The meaning separates itself from the "referent" (of the designated world) and installs itself in the mind of the speakers, carried there by the mental image of the sounds. The interaction that permits language—conversation—is so superior, in subtlety as well as efficiency, to all that has preceded it that it becomes the human activity par excellence, influencing all other forms of interaction. Language itself is social because it comes to us from other men who have preceded us, and its acquisition establishes the final and irreversible entrance of the child into existence. This acquisition also has many stages and, in a sense, never ends.

We can now review these stages to try to identify the elementary forms of interaction that the infant progressively acquires. This identification will be, in a way, a basic vocabulary from which we can derive, by combining and transforming, the complex actions of adult life.

In the course of the first stage, that of contact, the activity that distinguishes itself from the simple physiological functions has been described by specialists with the help of different terms with related meanings. Infants look for comforting contact with a soft, warm body; they "desire" to be held, cradled, enveloped by sounds and odors, which will become familiar. They want, as is sometimes said in visibly projecting onto them an adult viewpoint, to be protected and reassured; they need attachment and tenderness. Here we have a primary behavior that does not replace something else or hope to obtain a result; it is an end in itself, which has sometimes been attributed to the *clinging instinct*. I will speak of all of these related actions in which the infant is patient and not agent as *being comforted*.

The second stage, that of the gaze, does not begin with the act of looking—the infant performs this act from the time he is born—but by the fact that he looks for the gaze of another; he wants to be looked at. The difference between the two is essential and marks the first important separation between man and other superior animals. These last, as we have already seen, experience the face-to-face situation but only in limited and late instances; it is absent in infancy. The young monkey, like a human baby, feels a need to be comforted. When he plays alone or with his peers, he always stays close to his mother; he wants to be able to see her. But he does not seek her gaze; he does nothing to make *her* look at him in return. The human infant wants to be seen and not just to see (in the language of Sartre—who saw very well the integral role of the gaze—this characteristic amounts to: "My fundamental connection with the Other-as-subject must be able to be referred back to my permanent possibility of *being seen* by the Other").[16] The gaze of the parent is the first mirror in which the infant sees *himself*.

This decisive moment marks the simultaneous birth of his consciousness of others (who must look at him) and of himself (the one others look at), and through this experience the birth of the conscience itself. Although he obviously cannot *say* so to himself, from this moment on the infant *knows, I* am looked at, therefore *I* exist; the gaze of the parent has introduced the infant into existence. As if they recognized the importance of this moment (when actually they do not), parent and child can look into each other's eyes for long moments, an action that will be very unusual at an adult age when a mutual gaze of more than ten seconds can only mean two things—that the two partners are going to fight or to make love. This decisive situation, in which the child is always patient and not agent, can be designated by the Hegelian term: He asks *to be recognized*.

During this same stage, between two and five months of age, the infant also begins to take on more active roles by participating in real exchanges with his parent. According to whether the two perform the same action, for example, making alternating sounds or gestures (which seems to be the most frequent), or perform simultaneous ones, two actions can be identified that will later become more precise—*alternating* and *cooperating*.

At the third stage, that of manipulation, relationships between people are relegated to the background, and the child tries especially to profit from his growing capacity to seize and move the objects around him. However, the distinction between people and things is not yet well established in his mind; he can act in the same way with human beings around him. Two activities can be identified here, *exploring* the surrounding world without changing it, and *determining*, becoming the active cause of changes in the world. These attitudes will meet with different developments in the adult world—exploring leads to knowledge, determining to the technique—but also in the human world to social action.

In the fourth stage, that of memory, actions appear. The child now tries to *imitate* his parent or his companion (the two were not well separated during the exploring or determining phase). Some time later, but always at the heart of this same stage, the child begins to *combat* his rivals. This action, which we have seen the classical philosophers—from Hobbes to Nietzsche and through Hegel—declare the fundamental characteristic of humanity, is far from being the first that the infant practices. In fact, it already implies an advanced development, and thus it appears equally difficult to speak of an innate aggressivity or a sadism present from the beginning. Michael Balint says that, in analysis, "we have never really seen a congenitally wicked or evil person, nor a real sadist. . . . It is suffering that makes one wicked."[17] Combat is an activity determined by its goal: to obtain an object or the attention of a person. The combat does not take place if no rival presents himself. Therefore, it is misleading to postulate in man an instinct or a drive or an energy of aggression; it is to reify as an innate quality, as a motivating principle, that which is only a means to an end. Contrary to what certain popularizations of ethnology lead us to believe, animals do not possess the "aggressive instinct" either.

Combat is the first action directed only toward companions, not parents. The latter are not rivals; hostility with respect to them cannot take the form of combat (but rather of sulking or, later, of revolt). Combat is not necessarily linked to a demand for recognition on the part of the rival. Instead, it is a test of strength. Two children fight over the same toy; the strongest will snatch it away without caring about the gaze of the defeated. Later, the combat might be accompanied by a demand for recognition by a third party, a spectator or judge. This combination of elementary actions leads to complex feelings such as jealousy, envy, or hate.

The acquisition of language during the fifth stage adds new dimensions to each of the earlier actions. It is now possible to be comforted or recognized with the help of words rather than gestures or looks. The world can be determined and explored in this way, in alternating words and in imitating them. We can also place at this time the so-called "oedipal" configuration. As Balint notes, it is different from earlier relations in three ways: 1) it is triangular instead of dual; 2) it is conflictual rather than complementary; 3) it is verbal rather than corporal.

Among these elementary actions, I have not mentioned love, because it seems to me that the relationship of the child to the parent gains nothing by being enveloped by this overly general term. In the beginning, the child feels a need of others, a need to be comforted and recognized, a need to enter into collaboration. Later, when the parent is recognized and identified, all the former ingredients meet once again. The love of the child is a composite and not a single basic action. The same could be said about the erotic love of adults, even though the two are not of the same kind. Sensual pleasure, a need to be acknowledged and to acknowledge others, to cooperate and to combat, all of these elements and many other things form an amorous relationship.

There exists, on the other hand, another simple action that parents and children discover a little later (and which itself can be an ingredient or a form of love). It could perhaps be called *being united*. The mother can very early have a feeling of communion with her child, a sort of mental equivalent of the intrauterine symbiosis. But one must wait longer for the *two* individuals to have the same feeling and not to confuse it with an illusion of returning to symbiosis. In the communion, one is not ignorant of the fact that the other is other; one remains inside a coexistence, but there is at the same time continuity between the two partners. This experience is absolute certainty, allowing for no doubt that one is accepted by the other. The two persons participating in this state understand what Aristotle attributed to friendship at its most perfect, the joy of one is the joy of the other, or rather, the simple presence of one, of whom one demands nothing, for the other is the source of a quiet joy. I love him for himself and not for me, rejoicing in his existence with no expectation of recompense. I have no need of it. To love in this way gives me an intense and expanded sense of my own existence. Original incompleteness is forgotten.

The relation of children to parents is marked by two transitions: when the children become adult and when the parents become old. At the moment children reach maturity, their position, as well as that of their parents, is transformed. We have seen that certain elementary actions were symmetric, others asymmetric. It is these last that find themselves especially affected by this transformation, for the roles of the parent and the child are radically different: one reassures and recognizes; the other is reassured and recognized. This difference in roles is what the child who has become an adult no longer wants to admit. With regard to comforting, the need to be protected and reassured is now seen as specifically infantile. An adult can sporadically need various forms of comfort, but if he feels a constant need for it, he will be considered by his fellows as ill adapted mentally. The growing child, precisely in order to feel like an adult, needs to reject the comforting offered by his parents ("I'm not a child anymore. Stop mothering me!"). The same does not apply exactly for recognition; we always need it, as a child or as an adult, but in the place of the almost mechanical comforting offered by the parents, the growing child now wants a multiplicity of new acknowledgments from his peers, from the beloved person, from professors, and from superiors at work and so on.

Not only does the child who is now an adult no longer want to be the beneficiary of comfort and recognition coming from parents, he also wants to assume the active role in these relationships and, in turn, become the source of protection and recognition. For he now understands that, if there is an advantage in being comforted and recognized, there is another much greater one in lavishing comfort and recognition on others (we could have observed the embryo of this new attitude the moment the child refused to recognize his own parent, preferring to sulk and thus punish him or her for an earlier lack of attention). However, it is not with his parents, able-bodied adults who are used to doing without this kind of care, that he can practice these new roles. He inevitably turns away from them, searching for new situations in which these roles will be available to him.

The experience of the parent is obviously different. The love of parents for their child has a paradoxical side in its very nature. If they love their child, they want him to become an independent person who, as a consequence, has no need of them; the "successful" love of the parents has the effect—painful—of estranging their child from them. Individual memory, possessed by mankind to a degree unknown in animals, makes a perfectly common experience of separation from the children painful (after a time, the mother monkey does not even know her children from the children of others). This paradox of human parental love becomes clear at the moment when children become adults and can do without earlier comforting and recognition. The parents finds themselves suddenly deprived of the role of protector and the source of recognition, a role that could be at the roots of their own mental equilibrium. This predicament is the "empty nest" syndrome. In the best cases, a give-and-take relationship replaces the preceding asymmetric one, but we cannot say that one truly compensates for the other. The loss of children, since they are no longer children, is, in a sense, irreparable. The communion with the child can never again be possible in the same way.

The relationship that links parent and child contains from the beginning both symmetric and asymmetric aspects. What the two have in common, as Alice Balint has pointed out, is that neither of the two partners really acknowledges the autonomy of the other. She suggests that for the mother in particular, to a certain degree the child remains forever a part of her body, and mothers do not experience infanticide as a murder (but rather as an amputation). Reciprocally, the child expects that his parent will always be available, that there is nothing in life that counts more than himself, that the parent loves and accepts him no matter how he behaves. Michael Balint describes the feeling of the child for his mother in this way: "I must be loved, always, everywhere, in every way, in my entire body, in my whole being—with no criticism and without the least effort on my part."[18]

The differences, however, are even more important. The child can have only one mother and father; the adults can have this child or another. The parents are indispensable to the child; the child is not to the adults. In addition, the child lives with his parents at the time his interior psychic configuration is formed, while the reverse is not true. As a consequence, the role each plays in the psyche of the other is very different. For the children, the parents will never leave their *internal universe*, since the relationships with them make up its very foundation. On the other hand, when the children become adults, the parents normally leave their *life* and do not return to it until much later when, because they are approaching death, they must be taken care of. For the parents, on the other hand, it is not their children but their own parents who play a role in structuring the psyche, and when the children become a part of their life, an ingredient in their identity, they remain so forever, whatever the concrete relationships they maintain with them.

The second decisive transition in relations between children and parents takes place when the parents become old. The most obvious change in their life consists in they themselves becoming the ones who need care. They sometimes need to be fed, washed, kept warm, or helped to move about. In a word, they are now as dependent as the tiny child once was, and they need, in their turn, to be comforted. In a good number of cases, they find it necessary to have help, sometimes even from their own children, but even if it happens that they are comforted, they never again have the opportunity to console others, especially their own children. It is the same for recognition. They can continue to be recognized by those close to them, but no longer will anyone ask them for recognition; their gratitude is all that is expected. Their position regarding those who look after them, let us say their children, is as asymmetric as was that of children—beneficiaries but not givers of comfort and recognition (or not the right kind). With one important differ-ence—the child does not know in the beginning that he himself will one day have the strength to comfort and to acknowledge and that the benefit he will derive from this function is more substan-tial than the one he enjoys in his passive position. The old person knows that the active role is much more gratifying but also that he will never again have access to it. The tragedy of old age is not that you need others but that others no longer need you.

In supposing that they will become the guardians of their own parents, the children, who are now adults and themselves ap-proaching old age, can receive a supplementary gratification from this inversion of roles. They can be happy in providing for the well-being of a person dear to them. But the aging and the death of their parents will probably also have another effect. In today's society, when children become adults, they prefer to keep their parents at a distance, preferring to escape the gaze of those on whom they were entirely dependent. In the universe of childhood, it is the parents who exercise sanctions and, even as an adult, I cannot forget my past position. As long as my parents live, I remain, in a way, a child—for them but also for myself. This feeling can have contradictory effects. On the one hand, I would like to maintain this situation, because it allows me to avoid total responsibility for what happens to me (the child's privilege). On the other hand, however, and perhaps in a more intense manner, I want it to end and, therefore, hope for the death of my parents, for it is only from this moment on that I cease to be a simple fragment in another's universe and no longer have to dread the sanctions they might impose on me. The dependency on others cuts both ways; that of the child who has become an adult in relation to his parent can be more a weight than a gratification.

A good interaction between the child and his parents or with those who replace them is by all accounts largely responsible for his mental health, present and future. To have had during his in-fancy the certainty of being loved in this unconditional way that children demand of parents later allows the adult to face the trials that await him in life with more serenity. This initial attachment, Bowlby insists, is the only solid basis on which a personality can be constructed. As everyone knows, however, the accidents that await the individual on this path are innumerable, and the path of "good interaction" is not easy to find. Therefore, all the authors of the British school of intersubjective psychoanalysis have set about distinguishing different types of dysfunction in initial relationships that eventually become sources of pathology in adulthood. For example, Balint has psychoses go back to the first connection between the child and its mother, the psychoneuroses to a later one with the father and the mother. Melanie Klein contrasts the "good objects" that leave us and cause depression with "bad objects" that become part of us and provoke a feeling of persecution. Fairbairn distinguishes the schizophrenic child, who is afraid to love, from the depressed child, who is afraid to hate. Guntrip speaks of the possessive mother (who wants to be everything to the child) and the indifferent mother (who wants to be nothing).

Having no professional experience in the area of mental pathology, I will not try to evaluate the clinical importance of these typologies. But it seems certain to me that the malformation of any of the elementary activities previously pointed out might later bring on psychic disturbances. However, the most decisive role seems to stem from the first two interactions of the child, being comforted and being recognized. As a consequence, their disruption has very serious after-effects.

Such a disturbance will follow two paths: comfort and recognition can be either absent or present but not appropriate to the child's demand. Their simple absence produces predictable (and serious) results. Such is the case also with the fear that this absence will happen, a fear that ends in a feeling of dread. Harmful presence can also take different forms. One is that which we associate with the possessive parent who not only reassures and recognizes his child but also does not want anyone else to do so. He wants to be the only one to satisfy all the "social" needs of the child, leaving no place for a third person. This temptation is especially strong in a parent who raises his child alone and who is intoxicated with his own omnipotence.

Another destructive kind of recognition is one the parent offers hoping to see in the child another well-defined person, either absent or dead. Many parents who have lost a child during a war have another one as soon as peace returns, and they do all they can to make the new arrival resemble the picture they have of the earlier one. They give him the same name, the same bedroom, the same clothes, and believe they see in him their resuscitated firstborn. Other parents project onto the child the image of a dead brother, a lost lover, or even a famous man they especially admire. The child is recognized, but he understands immediately that he is taken for another. There is a risk that existence may take place for him in a kind of inauthenticity or even imposture. He will never know if he himself is really speaking from his own mouth, if he has made himself worthy of the one his parents wanted him to be.

The evolution of the child does not lead from a total dependence to an equally total independence but rather, as Fairbairn has suggested,[19] from a suffered dependence, whose actors and their rhythm of presence and absence are not of his choosing, toward an adult dependence, where he has a no less imperious need of others but where the different forms of recognition are not all concentrated in a single person and where he knows how to savor moments of solitude, where the relations come not only from the accidents of destiny but also from choice, where one can himself give them a beginning and an end.

3 Recognition and Its Destinies

It is not by chance that, of all the elementary processes, Rousseau, Adam Smith, and Hegel have emphasized recognition, which is unique in two ways. First, by the content itself: More than any other action, it marks the entrance of the individual into specifically human existence. It also has a structural singularity, however, since it is, in a way, the necessary companion to all other actions. In fact, when the child participates in actions of alternating or cooperating, he also receives confirmation of his existence in that his partner makes a place for him, stops to hear "him sing," or sings with him. When he explores or transforms the world around him or when he imitates an adult, he understands that he is the subject of his own actions and is, therefore, a being who exists. When he is comforted or fought with or when he shares with another, he also receives as a secondary benefit, the proof of his existence. All coexistence is a recognition, and thus I attach more importance to this process than to any other.

It is clear that recognition encompasses innumerable activities of the most varied kind. Once such an all-inclusive idea is introduced, we must ask what are the reasons and forms of this diversity.

To begin with, several sources of this diversity can be found external to the idea itself. Recognition can be material or nonmaterial; it can be wealth or honors and may or may not involve the exercise of power over other people. The longing for power can be conscious or unconscious, setting in motion rational or irrational mechanisms. I can also try to attract the gaze of another person by different facets of my being, my physical appearance or my intelligence, my voice or my silence. From this standpoint, clothes play a special role, for they are literally a meeting place for the other's gaze and my wish, and they allow me to situate myself in relation to these others. I want to look like them, or like certain ones but not like everyone, or like none of them. In short, I choose my clothes according to others, even if it is only to let them know they mean nothing to me. On the other hand, whoever can no longer be in control of what he wears (because of poverty, for example) feels paralyzed in the face of others, deprived of his dignity. An old joke, that a human being is composed of three parts, soul, body, and clothes, is not entirely mistaken in this case.

Recognition touches all the spheres of our existence, and its different forms cannot be substituted for one another. At most they might, if need be, offer some consolation. I need to be recognized on a professional level as well as in love and friendship, but the faithfulness of my friends does not truly make up for the loss of love, any more than the intensity of private life can erase a failure in politics. An individual who has invested the largest part of his demand for recognition in the public sector but no longer receives any recognition for this finds himself suddenly deprived of existence. Such a man has spent his life serving society and the nation, and it is from these entities that he receives the essential part of his feeling of existence. When old age has come and social demands disappear, he does not know how to balance this loss by the attentions of those close to him. Since he no longer exists in a public way, he simply has the impression of not existing at all.

We have seen with Hegel that the demand for recognition could accompany a struggle for power, but it can also be linked to relationships where the presence of a hierarchy allows conflicts to be avoided. The superiority or inferiority of partners is often known in advance, but each still hopes for the approval of the other's gaze.

The first recognition the infant receives comes from those who are superior in the hierarchy, his parents or their substitutes. Later, the role is taken over by other agents that society has appointed to exercise this function of sanction: teachers, professors, employers, directors, or bosses. Critics often hold the key to recognition for beginning artists and writers or for those among them who lack personal confidence. Society gives all of these superiors the essential function of bestowing public approval.

Even recognition coming from inferiors is not to be ignored, even though it is most often concealed. It is well known that the master needs his servant no less than the reverse, the professor is given a feeling of existence by students who depend on him, every evening the singer needs the applause of admirers, and parents are traumatized by the departure of their children, who had seemed only to be asking for recognition.

These hierarchical varieties of recognition resist as a whole the egalitarian situations in which feelings of rivalry are more readily apparent. These situations are many—love, friendship, work, part of family life. Finally, it is possible for one to become the only source of recognition for oneself, either by taking the path of autism in refusing all contact with the outside world or by developing inordinate pride and reserving for oneself the exclusive right to appreciate one's own merits, thus ultimately arousing in oneself an incarnation of God that serves to approve or disapprove of our conduct. In this way the saint tries to overcome his need of human recognition and be content with doing good. Certain artists can also devote themselves to their work without caring what others think of them. We must add, however, that such solutions are never anything but partial or temporary. As William James has noted: "*Complete* social unselfishness, in other words, can hardly exist; *complete* social suicide hardly occur to a man's mind."[1]

We must now distinguish two forms of recognition to which we all aspire but in very diverse proportions. They could be called a recognition of *conformity* and a recognition of *distinction*. These two categories are opposites: either I want to be perceived as being different from others or as being like them. The one who hopes to demonstrate he is the best, the strongest, the handsomest, the most brilliant wants to be distinguished from others, an attitude especially frequent during youth. But there also exists a very different type of recognition that is more characteristic of childhood and later of maturity, especially in people who do not lead an intense public life and whose intimate relationships are stabilized. They draw their recognition from conforming as closely as possible to the customs and norms that they consider appropriate to their condition. These children or adults consider themselves satisfied when they dress suitably for their age group or their social milieu, when they can brighten their conversation with appropriate references, and when they prove their unfailing attachment to a group.

If, by my work, I take on a function that society considers useful, I can overlook not having a recognition of distinction (I do not expect people to shower compliments on me). I am perfectly content with my recognition of conformity (I do my duty, I serve my country or my company). To have this recognition, I do not need to repeatedly solicit the gaze of others. I have internalized this gaze in the form of customs and norms and possibly of snobbishness, and just my conformity to rules supplies me with an image—positive, moreover—of myself. Therefore, I exist. I no longer aspire to being exceptional but rather to being normal. The result, however, is the same. In appearance, the conformist is more modest than the vain man, but he needs recognition no less than the other.

The satisfaction derived from conforming to the norms of the group also explains in great part the power of community feelings, the need to belong to a group, a country, a religious community. Scrupulously following the habits of a milieu furnishes you with the satisfaction of feeling that you exist because of the group. If I have nothing to be proud of in my own life, I am more determined than ever to prove or defend the good renown of my nation or my religious family. No reversals suffered by the group can discourage me. A man has only one existence and it can be spoiled, but a people has a destiny stretching back centuries; the failures of today can be the forerunners of the triumphs of tomorrow.

These two forms of recognition can easily conflict with each other or form shifting hierarchies in the history of societies as well as of individuals. Distinction favors competition; conformity is on the side of agreement. Will I wisely wait on the edge of the sidewalk to obey community rules and offer myself the internal recognition of conformity? Or will I cross the street in the middle of roaring cars to provoke the admiration of my pals (a recognition of distinction but one that can also become a recognition of conformity within a restricted group, that of our band of friends)? At a certain age the approval of our peers is worth more than anything else and certainly more than the satisfaction of conforming to general rules of society. This situation contains many dangers. It is easy to go against "morality" if one is sure of the laughter or amazement of onlookers. Crimes committed in a group often have no other incentive.

Another distinction is no longer concerned with forms of recognition but with the process itself. Recognition actually contains two stages. What we demand of others is, first of all, to recognize our existence (*recognition* in its narrow sense), and, second, to confirm our value (let us call this part of the process *confirmation*). The two desired interventions are not located at the same level; the second one takes place only if the first one has already occurred. When someone tells us that what we are doing is good, this compliment implies that he has already acknowledged our existence beforehand. Confirmation concerns the predicate of a clause; recognition is its subject (or an underlying clause that has the form of X, a pure clause of existence). La Rochefoucauld is perhaps one of the first to have distinguished the two: "We would rather speak ill of ourselves than not at all,"[2] he wrote. Adam Smith is equally aware of this duality, of the difference between "attention and approbation,"[3] and he already puts us on guard: "To be overlooked, and to be disapproved of, are things entirely different."[4]

In reciprocal fashion, the admiration of others is only the loudest form of their recognition, for it concerns our value. Their hate or aggression is also recognition, however, if in a less evident fashion, and it bears witness no less forcefully to our existence.

The distinction between these two degrees of recognition is essential, for they are often found dissociated and provoke specific reactions. We can be indifferent to the opinion others have of us, but we cannot remain insensitive to a lack of recognition of our very existence. As William James has pointed out, "persons for whose *opinion* we care nothing are nevertheless persons whose notice we woo."[5] Contemporary psychiatrists also recognize two forms of failure, each with different implications: *rejection*, or lack of confirmation, and *denial*, or lack of recognition. Rejection is a disagreement on the contents of the judgment, while denial is a refusal to acknowledge a judgment has been made, and here the offense to the subject is much more serious. Rejection is like a grammatical negation affecting only the predicate, and in fact implies a partial confirmation of the contents of the clause, the part borne by the subject.

Moritz has pointed out this difference in observing the opposite effects of derision and hate. "To be made ridiculous is a kind of annihilation, and to make a man ridiculous is a kind of murder of self-confidence. On the other hand to be hated by all is, in comparison, a thing to desire. Thus universal hatred would not destroy self-reliance, but give it new strength to live for centuries and gnash defiance at the world that hates. But to have no friend 'and not even to have an enemy' is true hell, which sums up in itself all the tortures which the sense of nonentity inflicts on a thinking being."[6] The hatred of someone means his rejection and can, therefore, reinforce his feeling of existence. But to make fun of someone, not to take him seriously, to condemn him to silence and solitude is to go much further; he then sees himself threatened with nothingness.

Dostoyevsky has made the difference between these two experiences—the refusal of confirmation (rejection) and the refusal of recognition (denial)—one of the principal themes of his *Notes from the Underground*. The feverish narrator of this story dreads denial above all else but willingly accepts rejection because it proves, although in a disagreeable manner, his existence. For example, he meets an officer who pretends not to see him. He dreams of having a fight with him, all the while knowing that he will be easily beaten. He does so not out of masochism, but because to fight someone implies that this person has noticed your existence. The officer, for his part, does not want to condescend to this interaction. When the two meet in the street and the narrator blocks his path, the officer refuses to fight: "He took hold of me by the shoulders and without a word of warning or explanation, moved me from where I was standing to another place, and he went past as if he hadn't even noticed me."[7] The same logic is at work in the relations of the narrator and his other acquaintances. Provided his existence is acknowledged, he is ready to accept the most humiliating situations; the most insulting words are better than the absence of any recognition. If being a slave assures us of the gaze of others, this condition becomes desirable. The underground man—and here he speaks the truth about all men—does not exist outside of the relations with others; not to be is a misfortune more dreadful than being a slave. Therefore, "to plunge into society" becomes for him "an irresistible urge";[8] to be alone is not to be at all.

The humiliation felt in both cases is not the same. Rejection can be negotiated either by an analysis similar to that of the underground man or by simple pride. What does the opinion of others, whom I disdain, mean to me (those grapes are far too green)? It remains true, however, that certain rejections are difficult to endure. To be ignored gives us the feeling we are being annihilated and causes suffocation.

We have seen that recognition is an asymmetric relationship. The agent gives recognition, the patient receives it; the two roles are not interchangeable. However, we have also seen that all other elementary actions bring, at the same time, a secondary or indirect recognition, owing not to the gaze of another but to the simple fact that we find ourselves taking part in an interaction. This fact also applies in the relationship of recognition itself. The agent of a direct recognition receives the benefits of an *indirect* recognition by the very fact that he plays his role. To feel necessary to others (to accord them recognition) means that one feels oneself recognized. As a general rule, this indirect recognition is more intense than the direct one. In the Warsaw ghetto, recounts Marek Edelman, a survivor, the surest way to survive was to devote oneself to another: "Everybody had to have somebody to act for, somebody to be the center of his life."[9] The parent who devotes himself to his child suffers more on the day when he feels the child has no more need of him than during the period in which he gave without ever feeling he got anything in return. In addition, indirect recognition escapes our moral censure, which is always quick to condemn anyone who asks too openly for praise. To be strong, to support and encourage others brings its own gratification, but to call for help implies that we are admitting our vulnerability and weakness, an appeal that is more difficult if one is neither an old person nor a child, neither a sick person nor a prisoner.

The choice between the different modes of recognition does not depend entirely on the situation at hand or on the will of the individual. Certain societies and certain periods favor one and exclude another. Here an important question must first be examined: Is the desire for recognition truly universal, or does it only characterize Western society, the only society I have spoken of until now? When Rousseau speaks of the "universal desire for a reputation, for honors, and for special treatment," is he not projecting the features of the society in which he lives, or of those that have preceded and prepared this society onto the entire planet? Is this viewpoint not a consequence of what the followers of other traditions, Buddhism, for example, have always criticized in Europeans, that is, their excessive preoccupation with the ego's well-being?

And even in the heart of Western civilization, does this description not apply much more to a worldly and public life than to the anonymous and peaceful one of simple folk, of laughing children, of young girls who dream, of fishermen who meditate with their lines in the water, or of peasants who work the soil? Finally, in the decisive text for the Western tradition, the Gospels, is it not explicitly stated that we must not act "in public to attract attention," "to win human admiration," but content ourselves with the knowledge that our Father, "who sees all that is done in secret,"[10] will know everything and will distribute rewards equitably?

What is universal, and basic to humanity, is that from birth we enter into a network of interhuman relationships, a social world; what is universal is that we all hope for a feeling of our own existence. The paths that allow us to gain this feeling, on the other hand, vary according to different cultures, groups, and individuals. Just as the capacity to speak is universal and basic to humanity but the languages are diverse, so sociality is universal but its forms vary. The feeling of existing can be the result of what I call fulfillment, the unmediated contact with the universe, as coexistence with others. This coexistence can take the form of recognition or cooperation, of combat or communion. Finally, recognition does not have the same significance depending on whether it is direct or indirect, of distinction or of conformity, internal or external. The desire for reputation, honors, special preference, even if it is always present, does not govern the totality of our life (it illustrates pride, not the idea of recognition). It is simply this realization that allows Rousseau to understand that there is no human existence without the gaze we direct toward each other.

Certainly, the question of social recognition does not take the same form in a hierarchical (or traditional) society as it does in an egalitarian one, such as modern democracies (Francis Fukuyama paved the way for a study of recognition from this perspective). In traditional society, the individual hopes rather to occupy a place that has been assigned in advance (his choice is more limited). If he finds it, he feels he belongs to an order and thus exists socially. The son of a peasant will become a peasant and will by this very act, acquire the feeling of being recognized. We can say, then, that recognition of conformity predominates here. This place to which one is predestined disappears in a democratic society, where the choice is theoretically unlimited. Not conformity to a certain order but rather success becomes the sign of social recognition, which is a much more disturbing situation. This race to success belongs to the recognition of distinction, but it is not unknown in traditional societies, where it takes the form of a desire for glory or honor and thus sanctions personal excellence. This path is the one chosen by heroes who aspire to special recognition for the exploits they accomplish. In modern society, this ambition has been transformed into a search for prestige. Success today is a social value that we hurry to make public, but prestige does not arouse the same feeling of respect as glory (we envy the most prestigious people, such as TV stars, more than we respect them).

On the other hand, egalitarian society offers equal dignity to everyone (Hegel would say it is the equality shared by former slaves), which traditional society, not founded on the idea of the individual, never does. All in all, traditional society favors social recognition, while modern society offers all of its citizens a political and legal recognition (everyone has the same rights as opposed to the system of privileges governing hierarchical societies) and, at the same time, emphasizes a private life of feeling and family. The need for recognition remains just as strong.

These days one often hears politicians formulating an ideal society in which we work less in order to have more free time and enjoy our leisure more. Such an idea, however, presupposes a hedonistic conception of man, an animal consumer of pleasures, which is far from the truth. It is not at all certain that leisure and idleness are favorable to the development of a person. The easiness of life does not count for much when weighed against the lack of existence. Human beings long for symbolic recognition infinitely more than they search for the satisfaction of the senses, and as Adam Smith has already stated, they are ready to sacrifice their lives for something as laughable as a flag. In work the individual obtains not only a salary, which allows him to live, but also a feeling of usefulness, of worth, and, added to this, the pleasures of conviviality. He is attempting to exist more than just to live. It is not certain that he will find all of this satisfaction in leisure, where no one needs him and where the human contacts made lack any necessity. Physical repose can be welcome, but the absence of recognition breeds anxiety. To give a sense and pleasure to work itself is without doubt more useful than multiplying the distractions.

Whatever the forms of recognition, one of the main characteristics should not be forgotten. Since the demand is by nature unending, its satisfaction can never be complete or definitive. With the best intentions in the world, parents cannot watch over their infant every minute. Others want their attention, and they themselves need other kinds of recognition, not only that which the baby indirectly offers them. Furthermore, the baby rapidly enlarges the radius of his appetite. Not only the parents but also visitors must give him all their attention. Moving on from one to the other, he demands attention from the entire world. Why should there be people who refuse to offer him their gaze? The appetite for recognition is appalling. As Freud has remarked jokingly on the occasion of his eightieth birthday, "You know, one can tolerate endless amounts of praise."[11] Even the recognition of conformity, more tranquil than that achieved by distinction, demands that the pursuit be repeated every day. Our incompleteness is not only basic, it is also incurable (otherwise we would be "cured" also of our humanity).

STRATEGIES OF SOCIAL DEFENSE

The recognition of our being and the confirmation of our value are the oxygen of existence. Since each person makes a similar demand, it is by definition impossible to satisfy them all. Other individuals also seek it and so are occupied and unable to respond to us. Put into practice, the request encounters indifference or refusal. The permanence of the request seems incompatible with the similarity between men. Thus a question arises: How do we manage failed attempts at recognition? I believe there is a manner of reacting that is more satisfying than the others and that takes into consideration the need we have of others along with the plurality of subjects who experience it. But there are also many other ways, familiar to all of us, that conceal or put off the frustration we feel without curing it and, in addition, even add a new one. These ways should be identified as *palliatives*, which the dictionary tells us "reduce the symptoms of an illness without attacking the cause." They are temporary expedients with only temporary effect.

All the specialists of the human psyche find themselves obliged to introduce a comparable idea, corresponding to the protections we have at our disposal, even if they do not agree on the exact function that these ideas assume, since these specialists do not see our mental life in the same light. Adler, for example, speaks of *compensations* that we produce to conceal our feeling of inferiority (a disconcerting name that he gives to original incompleteness). Freud, starting with his image of isolated man looking for maximum pleasures, uses the image of *sedatives*: "Life, as we find it, is too hard for us; it brings us too many pains, disappointments and impossible tasks. In order to bear it we cannot dispense with palliative measures,"[12] and he reminds us of a comparable expression of the poet, Theodor Fontane: *Hilfskonstruktionen*, relief constructions. Sartre, in *The Words*, calls them the *balms*. Anna Freud, in a celebrated book, has listed the *mechanisms of defense* but limits herself here to the conflict between the ego and the id. The mechanisms, or strategies rather, that we will examine are turned outward; they govern our relations with other people.

Palliatives offer instant relief to our frustration, but in the long run they prove to be harmful. The reason is that they do not attack the root of the evil, and they are sooner or later unmasked by our own vigilant mind but not before having left undesirable after-effects or even worse; their disadvantages are greater than those of the disease they were supposed to cure. Sartre writes: "Generosity, . . . like avarice or race prejudice, is only a secret balm for healing our inner wounds and which ends by poisoning us."[13] It is surprising to see aligned in one series, avarice, generosity, and racism (or to see this last described as a "balm"), but such is the diversity of palliatives that the demands for recognition create. These same "balms," once they become ineradicable habits, can lead to neuroses or psychoses and demand, in their turn, new therapies. But the palliatives themselves are not part of the mental illness; we are in the domain of daily practice, in ordinary frustration rather than in pathology.

How can we organize the endless variety of palliatives, and in what order should we examine them? It is clear, first of all, that no pretension of an exhaustive study is claimed here. Our mind is always inventing new defenses once the old ones have been brought to light. I do not plan to follow the author of a small volume in the "Que sais-je?" series, in claiming there are no more, no less than twenty-seven "reactions formations of social defense,"[14] but I will restrict myself to mentioning in an informal manner certain palliatives that are especially frequent and powerful. On the other hand, it is appropriate to distinguish several groups among them that reflect the different components of the process of recognition. If my initial demand is not crowned with success, I have the choice of several solutions. Or I may attempt it again until I obtain satisfaction or else look for something easier to obtain (a sort of substitute recognition) in place of the recognition I asked for, or, finally, I can change the demand itself in order to be able to give it up. I will follow this order here, without giving too much importance to this question of classification. It is simply a question of choosing a course to follow.

OBTAINING SANCTIONS

A first type of reaction to the refusal of recognition consists in asking for it again, not seeing in this failure anything but a set of unfortunate circumstances and a chance to do better next time. After all, there are also satisfied requests! If I am a handsome enough boy and sure of myself, no girl will be able to resist me. If I have a bright enough mind and a will of iron, I can win every contest. If I am talkative and do not allow myself to be intimidated by the cameras, I can make the best impression during my moment on TV and be called back to appear the next day. There really is a person who wins, a fighter, a strong student, a real race horse, beautiful, rich and intelligent, CEO of a multinational or a media star!

The problem this first attitude poses—which obviously has its good sides—is that the performance must always be repeated, with everyone and at every moment, since only success brings satisfaction. It is a *flight forward*, fatally condemned to failure (but if the reprieve is long enough, this destiny can always seem enviable). Freud was rather pessimistic about this: "An unrestricted satisfaction of every need," he wrote, "presents itself as the most enticing method of conducting one's life, but it means putting enjoyment before caution, and soon brings its own punishment."[15] William James describes the inevitable disappointments of this kind of person: "There is a whole race of beings to-day whose passion is to keep their names in the newspapers, no matter under what heading, 'arrivals and departures,' 'personal paragraphs,' 'interviews,'— gossip, even scandal, will suit them if nothing better is to be had."[16] Constantly demanding recognition, this type of individual is himself stingy with regard to others. He is admired and flattered but little loved. His power is recognized, but at the same time he is considered arrogant and vain. Seduction is not sufficient to guarantee love, a brilliant career does not produce happiness; all success is necessarily relative. This experience is humorously related in a well-known fairytale from the Grimm Brothers, *The Fisherman and His Wife*, (which inspired *The Turbot* of Günter Grass). After having gotten a cottage, the insatiable Elsabella demands a castle, then a royal palace. She becomes queen, empress, and even pope. But after demanding to become God, she finds herself back in her miserable hut, seated on the chamber pot.

In his memoirs, Joubert describes Chateaubriand as a person entirely dependent on the recognition of others and who does not know how to give anything in return. He thinks this trait is the reason for his unhappiness. "He wrote only for others and lived only for himself, and because of this, his talent never made him happy because the source of the satisfaction he could receive from it was outside of himself, far away, changing and unknown."[17] Chateaubriand's talent was immense, but public taste changes; if recognition cannot come from admirers, the writer is forcibly condemned to failure. Chateaubriand had an infinite need of others, but he cared little about knowing whether or not they, in turn, needed him. He believed he had done his part toward society when he delivered his works to the public.

We desire success and yet we do not achieve it because we are handicapped from the beginning—poor, ugly, mentally slow—or because of bad luck. So we take to *violence*, which society stigmatizes under the name of crime. The recognition I cannot get willingly, I will take by force. Perhaps frustration does not suffice to explain all aggression, but it is certainly one of the most common conditions. The thief supplies an illustration of this attitude. To achieve the recognition accorded to wealth, he uses ways not accepted by society. The gang wars in large American cities are carried out in a search for "respect," another name for recognition. The higher one climbs on the ladder of crime, the greater the power one can show. This power brings with it the respect of other individuals, even if it fails to get that of institutions, depositories of social values.

It is unquestionably true that women and men do not have recourse to violence, and especially physical violence, in the same proportion, and it is also true that men give into violence more willingly at a certain age (the insurance companies know this fact very well). In other words, a biological predisposition, rather than cultural conditionings alone, influences the choice of certain palliatives. This predisposition does not mean that men, or young men, are burdened with an independent instinct not found elsewhere, but rather that their hormonal constitution pushes them to choose one way to overcome the frustration in preference to others.

He who does not receive the necessary recognition and finds no way to console himself can become a violent criminal. He can also look beyond his own case, however, and ask himself if this absence of recognition does not affect everyone like him, all the poor, all the blacks, all the untouchables, and if it is not, therefore, necessary to try to modify, eventually by violence, the rules of the game itself. Here individual crime gives way to social *revolt*. It is not a question of the same form of recognition in the two cases certainly, since the revolt aims to transform institutions in such a way that they give respect and recognition to those who lack them, while individual violence looks for a noninstitutional recognition. Freud is as pessimistic here as he was regarding the forward flight: "One can try to re-create the world, to build up in its stead another world in which its most unbearable features are eliminated and replaced by others that are in conformity with one's own wishes. But whoever, in desperate defiance, sets out upon this path to happiness will as a rule attain nothing. Reality is too strong for him."[18] I personally do not share this fatalistic point of view; the rules of life in society can be improved, as has happened many times.

A special case of recognition obtained by force is that of the sovereignty of the senses in Bataille or Sade. It is characterized not only by the method employed, which is violence, but also and especially by the result obtained, which is no longer the love or admiration of others or even their simple acquiescence to one's existence. This time it is through the submission of others, which can be taken as far as destruction, through the affirmation of my power over them and not the capturing of their gaze, that my feeling of existence is established. Alina Margolis, a survivor of the Warsaw Ghetto and a militant in humanitarian organizations, once asked: How can we explain why a Lithuanian guard or a Salvadorean soldier is not content just to kill, as they were asked to do, but take a visible pleasure in cracking the head of a baby against a tree or against the wall of a house? The response, if we want to offer one, would be to look for the reason in the delight that the exercise of unlimited power offers, to feel that the life of others is in your hands, to be able to torture them or kill them without feeling and thus have an intoxicating confirmation of your existence. This thinking probably also applies to the rapist. He gets much more pleasure from the triumph of his will, victorious over all resistance, than from any sexual satisfaction. It must be pointed out again that this path is chosen by men far more often than by women.

The indirect recognition that the submission of others brings can take more social forms, and it is probably at work in the psychology of *tyranny*, whether it is exercised on a national or a family scale. Shakespeare's Richard III says: "Since I cannot prove a lover . . . I am determined to be a villain."[19] To be the evil one, the rascal, the monster, implies that one is feared and thus recognized. Sartre has clarified this idea centuries later: "The tyrant scorns love, he is content with fear. If he seeks to win the love of his subjects, it is for political reasons; and if he finds a more economical way to enslave them, he adopts it immediately."[20] Karen Horney has even thought she observed an "antimony of ambition and affection," which would be that one "cannot step on people and be loved by them at the same time."[21] Richard III found also at the end of his adventure: "There is no creature loves me, and, if I die, no soul will pity me."[22] What a feeble consolation to say, "Bah! I love myself!"

However, during his reign we see a different picture. In the course of the play, Richard manages several times to make himself loved, beginning with Lady Anne, whose husband and father he killed! Stalin was loved and feared at the same time, Hitler also. And who does not know fathers of families who enjoy the affection of their children and wife and not just their submission? Perhaps the problem lies elsewhere: The tyrant is loved, but he cannot allow himself to love another. Like Richard, he can only love himself, and as a result, this love does not bring him much in return. To admit his love for another is also to admit his need and therefore his own vulnerability. But the image the tyrant wishes to have of himself is that of omnipotence. As described by Hegel-Kojève, he is the master who does not need the recognition of the vanquished. To rule others unconditionally, he must remain alone. The tyrannical father can console himself in the company of other petty tyrants like himself.

A RECOGNITION OF SUBSTITUTION

Tyranny is akin to violence in its methods, but it does not lead to the recognition initially desired. In other cases, the failure of the first demand provokes a real reorientation, a change of level, without causing a transformation of method. Take a class at school. The child has the possibility of capturing the attention of the teacher by being the best in the class. But what if he does not manage to do so, if this way seems to him clearly inaccessible? Another possibility is then open to him that will allow him to attract the attention of his master as well as of his comrades with as much if not more success: by raising a fuss, by preventing the other students from obeying the rules, by being the worst student since he cannot be the best. (Obviously, these two cases do not exhaust all the possibilities. Other children will simply not be sensitive to academic recognition.)

In place of official recognition, one is free to choose another, sanctioning the *transgression* of the common rule. This strategy, familiar to the "underground man" of Dostoyevsky, who prefers to draw the reproaches of others rather than suffer their indifference, extends far out into life, well beyond classrooms. It explains much "extravagant" behavior and many "hysterical" acts in everyday exchanges. We also see that the criminal can expect a double benefit from his act: a direct one by the desired reward he obtains and an indirect one by the attention he attracts after the crime has been committed.

Anton Reiser, Moritz's hero, suffers cruelly from being an insignificant person, lost in the crowd, similar to others, or else an object of fun for them. One day by accident, he becomes drunk, which draws many reproaches. To his surprise, however, he sees that the overall effect of the incident is positive. "Yet when he entered the choir next morning and his schoolfellows laughed at his pale distracted appearance, which arose from his debauch of the day before, he felt a curious kind of pride as though his drunkenness had been an exploit, and he even made as though the after effects still lingered, in order to attract attention."[23] "To make himself noticed by the bad aspect of his behavior" brought him "a secret satisfaction."

An entirely different kind of substitute recognition consists in finding pleasure by proxy, thanks to the attention, even the admiration, aroused by a famous person. Here it is a question of a kind of *idolatry*. All celebrities arouse this phenomenon of satisfaction by transference: members of the royal families, stars of the cinema or singers, famous sports figures, well-known authors and artists. In this way I console myself (without admitting it) for the mediocre life I lead. In noticing in detail all the distinctions my idol receives, I share his satisfactions, which I imagine are infinite. I delight in the luxury that surrounds him. This operation is like the magician who performs a sleight-of-hand in raising himself by his hair. I choose the idol in question, I beautify him by my admiration, and I then benefit from the reflection of his beauty. I enjoy his aura of dignity, and the recognition I give him reflects back on me. "In a way we contribute to fine deeds when we praise them whole-heartedly,"[24] wrote La Rochefoucauld. In addition all of these advantages are obtained without the slightest effort on my part. It is my idol who writes, who acts on the stage, or who is glorious on the field of battle. I am the one who enjoys the benefits. "Mental laziness becomes a virtue; one can at least bask in the sun of a semidivine being,"[25] says Jung when he describes this strategy.

Practicing hero worship also offers another advantage, however, a feeling that one belongs to a group, a prestigious one in our eyes, that of the star's admirers. In this sense the experience of hero worship approximates that of members of any group who draw a recognition of conformity from simply belonging. Meeting a brother—or a sister—admirer warms the heart; each is reassured in his or her conviction by the others. During the 1930s, a member of the Nazi party benefited both from the success of his idol and from the feeling of being part of the right community. The supporter of a sports team receives recognition as much by the successes of the team as by the satisfaction he or she receives from belonging to the community of its admirers. In all of these cases, I continue to behave like a magician or a conjurer; I benefit from what I myself have created, that is, the value of the community to which I belong.

The satisfaction of belonging to a group that we have not chosen cannot be considered a palliative. Everyone feels reassured about his existence in finding himself in a familiar framework and among his own kind. But this common feeling can also transform itself and become a battle. I give all my strength to assuring the victory of my group; I am even ready to take on the role of martyr, and I struggle against all the rival groups. This identification with the interests of the group assures me of an unchanging recognition. Such an exacerbated form of social conformism could be called *fanaticism* and reminds us of the examples, so frequent all around us, of religious or nationalistic fanaticism. Often, it is a matter of solutions of substitution; the power of Muslim fundamentalism today has as a condition the impossibility of individuals, in the countries concerned, to have access to any other type of recognition. The same is true of Serb nationalism, the only path left to a population deprived of its former ideological reference points and unable to commit itself to the road recommended by individualistic societies.

Fanaticism is always accompanied by the hatred of others who are different. The reverse of communal belonging is the exclusion and denigration of those who do not belong to the right community and their condemnation to the role of scapegoat in every critical situation. But the demand for recognition by the group to which I belong (which can also be a "minority") is not in itself blameworthy anymore than are the other forms of recognition. The countries of Western Europe live today in a time of individualism, but we must not forget that everywhere else in the world and at every other period of history the collective identity predominated.

Another form of substitutional recognition consists in entertaining the *illusion* of recognition. Here one does not give up looking for the recognition of others, and he does not believe that he can bestow it on himself. This time one imagines that others recognize him, when it is not true. The normal human being lives with his fantasies but distinguishes them from the real world; the mad person is one who can no longer free himself from his paranoia. "Each one of us," writes Freud, "behaves in some one respect like a paranoic, corrects some aspect of the world which is unbearable to him by the construction of a wish and introduces this delusion into reality."[26] Religion, for Freud, is one of the collective illusions. If one is not loved in this world, he will be in the next. The disadvantage of the recognition by illusion is certainly in the (always possible) test of reality, and the awakening can be painful. The writer, author of fictions, on the other hand, is well protected. He creates imaginary worlds that can bring him desired satisfactions, but he does not usually mistake himself for a character in the novel. Rousseau made this use of the imaginary programmatic, declaring it preferable in principle to reality. "I find my advantage better with the chimerical beings that I assemble around me than with the ones I see in the world."[27]

I can keep my illusions to myself. If I decide, however, to share them with those close to me, I enter into the category of *boasting*. The braggart believes he is communicating objective information; he does not see himself as the author of laudatory assessment about himself. In reality, tired of waiting for others to recognize him at his real value, he takes charge of the task himself and announces to those he meets, if not that he is praised and esteemed by all, at least that he is overworked, constantly demanded, that he does not have a minute to himself, that he has received flattering invitations that he cannot accept, that his last novel will be translated into thirteen languages, and so on. The more I produce signs of self-satisfaction, the more I emphasize my dependence in regard to others, since it is for their benefit that I present this idyllic picture. The declarations of contentment are really demands for love, and the hiatus between the two is somehow pathetic. This type of person is too well known for me to linger here; it is enough to point out that he belongs to the group of recognition by substitution.

RENUNCIATIONS

Certain forms of renouncing any pursuit of recognition are extreme. *Autism* is a serious ailment of the psyche that condemns a person to being walled up inside himself and refusing all contact, exchange, or communication with others. Whatever the origin of this disorder, organic or functional, the effect is the same: In refus-

to recognition being closed, they are all opened, or rather there is nothing but an opening. I become one with the universe and with life, so what does my tiny existence matter to me? To identify this state, Freud borrows an expression from Romain Rolland that speaks of an "oceanic feeling." Other psychoanalysts have thought they found here a reminiscence of the experience of the human embryo, the prenatal symbiosis. This acceptance of the entire universe, however, obliterates in its bosom the specificity of men; the fusion with others does not characterize the human condition, which is defined by separation and the feeling of incompleteness that results from it. The dream of symbiosis and fusion surreptitiously transforms another into a nonsubject and threatens him with being absorbed. Intrauterine existence could not possibly be the ideal of love; birth is only traumatic if one wants to escape the specifically human condition, which is made up of encounters.

These two forms of renunciation, although contrasting as nothing and all, resemble each other in their extremeness. Other renunciations are more moderate and, at the same time, more widespread. What I would like to describe under the name of *arrogance* is one of the most familiar. We can limit the sense of this word (in accord with many of its uses) to designate the renunciation of all confirmation of my value by an outside judgment and its replacement by a self-sanctioning, a confirmation that I alone have the privilege of giving. Arrogance is very different from boasting, even though here I also praise myself, because the arrogant person never lowers himself to share his appreciation of himself with others (he is too contemptuous of them to do so). Furthermore, arrogance does not necessarily demand self-flattery. I can be arrogant and severe with myself; the important thing is that I alone have the right to judge myself. The arrogant person is, therefore, very modest on the surface since he demands nothing of others. In this meaning of the word, he is not vain, but his self-esteem is much higher than that of the vain man who trusts the judgment of others. This phenomenon no doubt prompted Rousseau to write:

"Self-love, ceasing to be an absolute sentiment [that is, in entering into the social world], becomes pride in great souls, vanity in small ones."[29]

The arrogant person is one of the best possible approximations of the self-sufficient being. To avoid depending on others and thus admitting his incompleteness, he tries to know how to do everything himself. He is accomplished on the physical as well as on the mental level; he can always take care of himself. His desire for autonomy keeps him in good health, for illness means dependence. Or perhaps he is an ascetic person, devoid of needs. He eats little, lives a hard life. Christian saints have often been suspected of feeding an enormous arrogance. Anyone who says, "I don't need anything," also means I have everything; he dreams of himself as a god. In reality, arrogance makes us separate recognition of our existence from the confirmation of our value. I display indifference about this last but not about the former. I get my peace of mind, not from the positive judgment I have of myself, but from the fact that this judgment, positive or negative, is mine to make. However, I still have as much need of others to feel that I exist, even if I do not ask for their approval.

The arrogant person would like to present his activities as free from all outside purpose; he acts as though he is doing it because it is what pleases him the most in the world, not because he expects any reward. It is not that such a motivation is impossible in itself. Not everything we do is a search for recognition; we can also find a meaning in the accomplishment of even a gesture without having to receive an approving look for it. But in arrogance mediation is not absent; it is internalized. The distinction can appear specious, but it is nevertheless real. If someone—be he a cabinetmaker or a writer—does his work well, he can find satisfaction either in the positive judgment he accords himself (the arrogant internalization of the judgment of others) or in the very act of doing it, without going through any mediation (what I call "fulfillment").

On the surface the arrogant person is agreeable to everyone

around him but deep down he is frustrating. He is agreeable because he does not bother us with his appeals, does not constantly demand our attention, and he does more favors than he asks of others. He behaves modestly, and the modesty of others is something that is greatly appreciated. If I am destined to live with him, however, I discover, as time goes by, the disadvantages of the situation, for he refuses to offer me any indirect recognition and will not admit his own incompleteness. If he has no need of me, what use am I? A person who depends on me may cause me worry and annoyance, but he gives me more than he takes from me; he makes me necessary. "We always need someone who needs us,"[30] says a Romain Gary character. This mother complains about the time her child takes up, another woman suffers at having to visit a prisoner, that man is exasperated because he must look after his sick father; the disappearance of these dependent persons, however, would nevertheless be a blow to their feeling of existence. The demand for recognition that others ask of me is in itself a recognition of me. The arrogant man makes no demands on me, he does not ask for my approval; he does not admit his weakness. He even tries to do everything better than his neighbors, to such an extent that they feel humiliated by comparison. In this sense, the vain person, unbearable on the surface, is much more agreeable. He constantly shows his need of me, as Adam Smith has already pointed out. The arrogant man is more respectable but more difficult to live with. The vain person who wants to please everyone is a man of pleasant company; it is easy to make him happy.

The solution, for those close to the arrogant man, would normally be to leave, but he would not stand for it, and he would let them know it. He controls them with a double constraint, demanding that they stay with him (to confirm his existence) but not asking them for any particular contribution and displaying instead his completeness (his self-sanction). He is like an old husband who is contemptuous of his spouse but cannot do without her because he has acquired the habit of speaking in her presence (rather than

have been a compromise; the public obviously had bad taste. Early praise fades quickly. Finally, he remains the best judge, which does not in any way mean the most self-satisfied. "As I fear nothing so much as self-deception and consider conceit fatal to intellectual development, I take unremitting care to *under* rather than *over* estimate my value, and put all my pride in humbling myself."[32] It is the one who sanctions who is favored here, not its object, even if it is the same person. The privilege he gets from this position more than makes up for the drawbacks of the situation described.

It is possible to compare arrogance (understood in the sense of self-sanction) to certain attitudes of *devotion*. The devout person, whether he practices Christian charity or humanitarian aid, presents himself as someone who asks for nothing, who is perfectly unselfish, and who offers to give of his money, his time, his strength without compensation. The beneficiaries will be the needy, the poor, the sick, the threatened. In reality, of course, this avowed selflessness is not the case. He performs an act approved by public morality and keeps for himself the benefits of indirect recognition, the best kind. The devoted person practices more or less consciously a simplistic psychology (which is certainly not a reason for asking him to give up his activities). He acts as though others needed only to live but not to exist, or to receive but not to give. In this way he prevents others from feeling necessary themselves, which they would have been if the devout person had shown his own incompleteness, if he had been more open about the needs of the generous giver that he is. Systematic devotion is a one-way attitude that will not allow reciprocity. Indian lepers, the starving Sudanese will never be able to help me; most of the time they do not even know my name or my face. We know from stories of the beneficiaries of charity that they are put in a very difficult situation; they are happy to receive life-sustaining help but unhappy because their existence has been weakened, since they are condemned to receive without being able to give. Here again is Anton Reiser, taken care of by charitable people: "It was really nothing but the humiliating thought of being a burden which depressed him. . . . Although every one counted him fortunate, the year which Reiser spent thus was at certain hours and moments one of the most painful in his life."[33]

Once more, it is the impossibility of living a life of indirect recognition, one that comes from generous acts of which we are the subject and no longer the object, that explains this failure. In being devoted to others, I do not ask for direct recognition, or if I do, it is of a third party (the public, spectators in some way), not from those I help. In addition there is another advantage: in being occupied with the needs of others, I forget my own, and the benefits the subject gets from this choice are not negligible. As the very devout narrator of Gary's *King Solomon*, a novel whose central theme is devotion, explains it: "Chuck says I would have been the first Christian, if that had been possible. But me, I think it's just pure egotism, and that I think about other people so as not to have to think about myself, which is the one thing in the world that scares me."[34] It is the same for his colleagues in the "sos Volunteers." Here is Ginette: "When she listened to all the tales of woe at the other end of the line it made her feel better, and helped her to forget about herself; like it says in religion, it's always a relief to think about people who are worse off than you."[35] The vocation of those who give professional help could be explained in the same way. "For instance, there are some psychiatrists who weren't loved when they were young or who had always felt ugly and rejected and who make up for it by becoming psychiatrists and taking care of young drug addicts or drop-outs and who feel important and are in great demand, . . . they get a sense of power, and that's how they cure themselves and get to feel more at home in their own skins."[36]

I end my listing of palliatives in speaking briefly of another form of denying recognition that allows us, at the same time, to obtain a recognition of substitution—that of deliberately playing the *victim*. As with arrogance, recognition is this time essentially the product of something that is inside me (my conscience). Different from the preceding cases, it nevertheless comes not from a feeling of my value but from my being the victim of others' neglect. As in idolatry, there is something magic here. The frustrations, the narcissistic wounds from which I might suffer, become sources of satisfaction simply by the strength of my will, since it allows me to occupy the position, actually a desirable one, of the victim. "When we confide in another, our principal motive is often a desire for sympathy or admiration,"[37] wrote La Rochefoucauld, thus putting an equal sign between the victim and the hero, two postures in the solicitation of recognition.

But why should this situation be desirable? Because it offers me, first of all, internal compensations that are far more important than the disadvantages I find in my everyday social relations. Moreover, in identifying myself with a victim who has been unjustly persecuted, I create for myself an inexhaustible credit with others, and this factor is much easier to make use of because it does not demand any real quality on my part, which is not true of arrogance. In fact, the opposite is true. The failures I suffer reinforce my position. I feel sorry for myself, and this self-gratification consoles me for all the reverses I suffer. *Recounted* misfortune is never confused with *lived* misfortune; one is the opposite of the other, for even if I still do not have a *partner*, I now have a *listener*. As Marina Tsvétaeva said in passing, "Who could speak of suffering without being enthusiastic, meaning happy?"[38] Even if I do not receive anything, everything is due me and thus makes me invulnerable. It must be added that in reality we don't aspire to suffering the fate of the victim but only to acquiring the status of one. The distinction fits the case, for the "victim" I speak of here is not generally animated by masochistic tendencies; he does not want to suffer at all. The evil that allows one to acquire this status usually happened in the past or somewhere else; the role is assumed only contiguously (those who practice devotion to real victims are often indirect beneficiaries of the sympathy offered to these victims).

The status of victim can also extend to groups inside a society or to entire populations, thus assuring them of the privilege of making claims or even of impunity. Since according to democratic ideology, everyone must have the same rights (the same dignity), anyone who can claim that he has had less than the others in the past can expect extra benefits in the present. Serb propaganda during the Yugoslav conflict counted a great deal on this line of reasoning. The Serbs were pictured as former victims who, therefore, had the right to compensations (to conquests).

In *Anthropology*, Kant mentions the possibility of feeling a *sweet pain*, "for example, of a widow who has been left well off and refuses to be comforted."[39] One has the impression that this woman really lived in Königsberg and that our philosopher knew her. The elements of the situation are the following: first, the widow is rich; her survival is not threatened. In this sense, she is not a true victim; she simply plays the role. She refuses the consolations, in this case, the attentions of the men who surround her. The position in which she finds herself is a comfortable one: She is a victim of fate whom the whole world pities and who obviously does not deprive herself of letting others know about it; after all, the solitary philosopher himself had heard about it. Why trade this position for the uncertainty of a new union in which she would risk not finding the appropriate recognition but in which she would not have the right to complain?

The voluntary victim prefers the possibility of demanding that his wishes be gratified. Adler reports the case of a young girl who chose to play the victim with her mother. "Another time this same mother asked whether this little girl would like to have coffee or milk for lunch. The little girl stood in the doorway and murmured very clearly, 'If she says coffee I will drink milk, and if she says milk I will drink coffee!'"[40]

We must add here that the satisfaction of the victim comes only partly from self-pity; another part is produced by the consciousness others must have of his lamentable situation. The little drama includes in principle three roles: that of the victim who complains, that of the guilty one (who has not given the expected recognition), and finally that of the witness-judge who listens to the grievances of the victim and announces that he is worthy of sympathy. This third role is often that of someone close—a member of the family, husband or wife, child or parent—a public prisoner of the same space as the victim and to whom the victim recounts his troubles; whereas it is the others, the outside world, the colleagues or the neighbors, who play the role of the guilty one. The family cell, however, permits the roles of witness and guilty one to be taken by one person—the mother tells her son, the husband his wife that he or she is the cause of his troubles. The victimization of oneself implies, by correlation, the culpability of the others. If the witness is the only other person present, it is he who must wear the hat. Thus he is blocked by a double demand that is impossible to satisfy, both the source of the unhappiness and its remedy. Pushed to the extreme, the "game of victim" leads to the destruction of oneself as well as of others.

TAKING TURNS

Let us ask now: Is there any way to enjoy recognition that would avoid the disadvantages of the palliatives? And if so, what is it? I think a way is generally available, even if practicing it is not always easy. It is possible to admit both one's own sociality and the subjectivity of others, to accept the *you* as being both similar and complementary to the *I*. We could call this mode *taking turns*. This formula, which etymologically signifies that we must wait our turn (the "role" is the roll on which a list of names is written), can be understood in a dual sense, implying, on the one hand, alternating (turn) and, on the other, distributing the roles.

Everyone must take his turn, a maxim that some people take literally. Since each asks recognition from his neighbor, you could, by alternating, render this mutual service (we have already seen that this ability to alternate is part of our common baggage from the age of six months). I listen to you, then you listen to me, and we begin again. Of course, this variant is the most mechanical form of taking turns, even to the point of caricature. An innocuous example can be observed around the sandpiles of public gardens, where the young mothers (and less often, the young fathers) bring their offspring to build sand castles, ditches, and tunnels. In order to recite the adventures of your own child, you must be ready to listen to those of the neighbor's child (taking turns, says François Flahault, "implies a letting go, a putting off").[41] She tells me her boy has fallen out of bed, that he has a big bump, that he almost cried, that he didn't want to swallow his meat that evening. I listen to her patiently (even if I do not register anything she says), and in this way give her, at the minimum, the recognition she is asking for, confirming her in her role as mother. Thus having accumulated a little credit, as soon as she closes her mouth I can open mine. I do not comment on the events I have just heard about except for a "yes" at the beginning. But I, in my turn, begin a story exactly parallel; my daughter was really impossible yesterday, she drove me crazy. The neighbor is obliged to listen to me.

In this oversimplified version of taking turns, we can speak of a benefit (by being patient I obtained recognition of action in my role as parent), but we must admit that it was minimal. The negotiations that political groups go through during an electoral period furnish us with a more complex example. Here too alternating takes place; this time it is my turn, next time it is yours. There are also what could be called reciprocal withdrawals, a possibility offered to collective bodies but not to individuals. I give up my place in the first district; the partner group does the same in the second. But in addition there are the negotiations, the discussions, the compromises, the search for a consensus, which can advance the two parties and for this reason are more enriching.

It proceeds differently in long-lasting groups, of which the couple man-wife is the most common example. Other than the fact that here there is usually a division of roles (the second sense of "taking turns"), the two members of the couple do not need a simplistic alternation, because they have made a discovery that is the foundation for a happy recognition: your need produces my recognition and vice versa. The very demand that you make of me, of knowing how to acknowledge your existence, brings me confirmation of my own. I am recognized as the one you need. And in your case, my demand for recognition does not aggravate you. The opposite is true; it even gives you an exceptional stature since you are the only one able to give it to me. Cooperation is more profitable to each of the two partners than their parallel selfish wishes would have been. Contrary to what the partisans of individualist psychology claim, the subject finds his reward in the existence of another, not in doing away with him. In making him exist, I assure my own existence.

At the root of all dialogue lies a contract of reciprocity. The words I address to another person are a sign of my existence, and at the same time they establish that of the other. They acknowledge the discontinuity and at the same time the similarity of our discourses. To listen to what someone says to me, I must be quiet, as he will be in his turn. Here is a complicated ritual that we all master without thinking about it. This contrast, however, can be easily broken. One of the ways it can be thwarted is surprising. It seems that explaining it, making the two protagonists conscious of it, suffices to make it not function as well as before. In reality the clarification is an indication rather than the cause of its inefficiency. The private sphere welcomes contracts as long as they remain tacit, the opposite of what happens in electoral agreements (public life is not subject to the same rules as private life, and these restrictions vary according to the cultures). If they must be made more precise through discussions and if—the last stage before breaking off—they must be finalized in writing, it is because the mechanism of reciprocity is already jammed; the impossibility of improvisation, as well as generosity, proves to be fatal to the couple. Because—and here is the reason for the blockage—the request I address to my partner brings him or her recognition but not necessarily the type desired. You only need my body, he (or she) retorts, not my mind, or the reverse. Or sometimes: you acknowledge me as the mother of your children and not as an autonomous human being. It is not enough to know that every request is also a gift; you must be offered what you need.

The assigning of a specific role to each person is the other meaning here of the expression "taking turns." We know how this technique allows us to calm the atmosphere in a group of children. Before, everyone wanted the same toy at the same time and everyone was frustrated, but creating specific roles allows everyone to feel satisfied: one will stand watch at the window, another will hide behind the door, a third will sound the alarm. If each has his role, his existence is recognized by the very fact that he plays it, and the recognition of one doesn't prevent that of another.

The assigning of stable roles, even if they are not permanent, explains how numerous relationships function—parent and child, teacher and student, employer and employee, idol and idol worshiper. In each case, the passive need to be recognized by someone satisfies the active need to recognize in the other and vice-versa. At the same time, in each case the satisfaction is only partial—the actor does not merge completely with the role. He would like to play several at the same time, or he tires of one and demands another, or he changes and what satisfied him yesterday disgusts him today.

Taking turns is therefore no panacea. It satisfies our needs for recognition for the majority of those who make up human society, but it is in itself partial and fragile. To begin with the necessity for reciprocity and allocation is preferable to all the palliatives against the failure of recognition because it is more real, but it does not arrange anything definitively. Taking turns means to reinvent and begin again at every moment; a past dialogue will not do for a present one. This reinvention is another way of realizing that humans exist only and always in time.

4   Structure of the Person

INTERNAL MULTIPLICITY

In describing the process of recognition and its more or less imperfect realizations, I have disregarded one of its dimensions that
adds still more to its complexity. When there is interaction between the *I* and another, much more than one relationship is
formed at the same time. To the present exchange is added former
exchanges, earlier or more recent, possible future exchanges—all
duly reflected in the mind of the person hoping for recognition.
These before-and-after encounters, as well as others, experienced
as if in a conditional mood or with an interrogative status, arrive to
orchestrate and transform the surface action. They have for correlation the internal multiplicity of the human person; several instances are always active in each of us.

But how do we identify and place them in relationship to each
other? Since time immemorial, wise men and experts on the human soul have practiced such distinctions. The human being is not
only fickle, changeable (in the diachronic), he is also multiple (in
the synchronic). Plato, Aristotle, and the Stoics distinguish diverse
functions, or levels, of being. Montaigne found being multiple and
a little chaotic. "Our actions are nothing but a patchwork. . . .
and we want to gain honor under false colors."[1] Pascal would
contrast the body and the mind, the heart and reason. La Rochefoucauld would describe the many stages on which the human
comedy is played out, with, in the heart, autonomous characters

such as Pride, Arrogance, Self-Interest, or the Passions. The Romantics would be fascinated by the dual portrait of man and his shadow, Dr. Jekyll and Mr. Hyde, by this "mysterious thing in the soul" that Melville speaks of, "which seems to acknowledge no human jurisdiction but, in spite of the individual's own innocent self, will still dream horrid dreams, and mutter unmentionable thoughts."[2] For his part, William James distinguishes between the "material self" and the "social self," between the "spiritual self" and the "pure ego." Today we are used to speaking of the unconscious and the conscious or, according to Freud's last conceptualization, of the ego, the id, and the superego. Fairbairn, who always sees things as intersubjective, adds to this "topic" several "objects" (that is, subjects other than the *ego*): the Object that excites, the Object that repels, the ideal Object. Jung speaks of self and ego, of anima and animus, of persona and imago.

We can observe another multiplication of internal proceedings of the mind in the process of self-knowledge. As Borges recalls (quoting Paul Deussen analyzing Hindu philosophy), there is here a possibility of infinite multiplication, "because if our soul were knowable, a second would be required to know the first and a third to know the second."[3] It is the same with the dialogues we carry on within ourselves, alongside, over, or under, the dialogue in which we are engaged with a flesh-and-blood interlocutor. In his brief essay called *Company*, Samuel Beckett illustrated this complexity of internal dialogue in a different direction. The person who produces the text that we read is alone, but he talks to himself. "A voice comes to one in the dark"[4]: so I am two, a voice, on the one hand, someone, a listener, on the other. But there is also another, the one in which the voice and the listener are next to each other, two emanations, let us say, of oneself. Therefore, three people. One can, however, also envisage the "Deviser of the voice and of its hearer and of himself."[5] Now there are four. Are these four all the voices that are present? Beckett wrote: "In another dark or in the same another devising it all for company,"[6] and he comments, "For why or? Why in another dark or in the same? And whose voice asking this? Who asks, Whose voice asking this?"[7] The self imagines a voice and a listener; the inventor poses the question, Who asks it? But it is still another who can only string these questions together. And who asks, Who asks it? Must we call this fifth arrival the author? The regression of knowing or stating instances, of a subject who makes of himself an object, is theoretically unlimited even if in practice the limit of intelligibility is quickly reached.

Each of these representatives of human interiority (and there exist innumerable other comparable attempts) is situated in its own perspective, which is why there are so many. Taking the interaction of self and the other as a point of departure, we must proceed with our own analysis and leave aside categories that raise other perspectives. It is the intersubjectivity of the person that preoccupies us here rather than his will or his reasoning, his ability to act or his emotions. The categories that I will propose should not be interpreted as a questioning of former theories, which can each remain pertinent from its own viewpoint, but more as being complementary to them. On the other hand, they are not definitive; they must instead be considered as a cartographic reading of a still little-explored territory. Some difficult problems of terminology are raised, it is true, for all the terms designating the different progressions of the human psyche have already been used and, therefore, stated by various theories or philosophies, none of which has adopted exactly our perspective. I will use the term *self*, rarely used in this sense in French and so relatively available, to designate the place where these interactions take place, and I will distinguish between several instances that occur competitively and at any moment, a little like the members of a council of ministers, who are many but each has, in spite of some overlapping, very specific functions, and whose number and conflicts are masked by the unity of decision represented by the prime minister. My guide here will not be a scientist or a philosopher but a novelist. I will try first to describe the structure of the person involved in an inter-

of her friend about her own desire, joining in a collusion with another instance, the "discretion" of Mademoiselle Vinteuil. This discretion will introduce a new phase to lessen the effect of the first—see us reading, she clarifies. Here we are involved with a first facet of the person that could be called the reflected self and more specifically the part of the self that is created in preparation and anticipation of the reactions of others to the action of the *I*.

As we have just seen, however, it does not appear alone; it is immediately in conflict with another instance that is active in the interior life of Mademoiselle Vinteuil—the desire she feels for her friend (and which, in my terminology, comes from "to live" rather than "to exist"). Mademoiselle Vinteuil also uses her ability to guess the reactions of her friend in a simpler way, to obtain, on the contrary, the demand of the desiring self (the anticipation of another's reaction can serve different masters). For example, the friend turns her back to the picture of the father. "Mlle. Vinteuil realised that her friend would not see it unless her attention were drawn to it,"[10] so she speaks of it in a careless way, and the result is immediately obtained. But she must have more, the desecration of the picture. She manages it easily with a provocation: "Oh! You wouldn't dare,"[11] she replies to the proposition of her friend, which has the immediate effect of making her do it.

A new aspect of self is shown in the moments when the two friends replay the sequences that are familiar: Mademoiselle Vinteuil conducts herself in accordance with the image of herself that she imagines the friend holds; she pronounces the phrases that the other expects to hear—what the two indulge in are "ritual desecrations," the replies are part of "liturgical responses." The words that one says, she has heard "used by her friend on some earlier occasion."[12] Here we are once more concerned with the reflected self of Mademoiselle Vinteuil, but this time with the retrospective side, that is, with what she thinks the other already thinks of her.

The principal tension of the scene at Montjouvain, however, is found elsewhere—not in the relationship of the two friends (they are in agreement between themselves) nor in the relationships with the reflected self, which are well circumscribed, but in another internal conflict that we have been able to note in passing, where "discretion" opposed "desire." It is the conflict between the "wicked" appearance of Mademoiselle Vinteuil and her "good" nature. "And perpetually," says the narrator, "in the depths of her being, a shy and suppliant maiden entreated and reined back a rough and swaggering trooper."[13] The "ingrained timidity" battles the "impulse towards audacity."[14] Let us try to sort out these two new characters a little.

First, the "trooper." Mademoiselle Vinteuil desires her lover, but it is not only this matter: to arrive at the "full realisation of her desire," she thought it was necessary to add "premeditated words."[15] The desiring self decided to ally itself with another instance, a self of facade defined by its immorality. Mademoiselle Vinteuil acts out vulgarity and sadism. She dons a mask to put on an act. She forces herself to "find the language appropriate to the vicious woman she longed to be," to adopt "a particularly shameful and seductive form of the wickedness she was striving to emulate."[16] The desiring self looks for pleasure; the self of the facade, in concert with it, looks for evil. But why in concert?

Because, as the vocabulary itself that the narrator uses indicates to us, the pleasure of the senses and moral evil seem to Mademoiselle Vinteuil inextricably linked; she believes that, in order to obtain pleasure, you must do evil. It is not that the evil produces her pleasure (she is not a true sadist); it is more that she thinks pleasure is an evil and believes, as a consequence, that evil must be a pleasure. "Sensual pleasure" seems to her "something bad, the prerogative of the wicked." "It was not evil that gave her the idea of pleasure, that seemed to her attractive; it was pleasure, rather, that seemed evil. [. . .] She came at length to see in pleasure itself something diabolical, to identify it with Evil."[17] But, because of this, she must pretend to be bad in order to enjoy it. In order to enter "the inhuman world of pleasure," she must "endeavor to impersonate, to identify with, the wicked."[18]

Who is responsible for this destructive equation? What we could call common morality, of Christian origin, which claims that pleasure is the work of the devil. Proust, who knew how to show the distant sources of present conflicts, brings to life the law as well as its transgression. We can easily imagine that if the social taboo weighing on pleasure were removed, Mademoiselle Vinteuil would have had no need to play the wicked one in order to give into it. If she has her friend spit on the picture of her father, it is not because the desecration in itself offers any pleasure; it is that she believes she must belong to the cast of evil ones, of cruel and irreligious beings, in order to have a right to pleasure. For Mademoiselle Vinteuil, this morality does not exist only outside, in the world, but it now has become a character of her internal universe, an inaccessible master who may or may not deign to give his approval and therefore his recognition also.

This instance is not the only intervention of this generalized other as commonly held opinion. In other respects, it allies itself with yet another instance of her being, with a core that comes from her earliest childhood, and beyond that, from her heredity, to form her archaic self. This core is what the narrator calls "her frank and generous nature."[19] In fact, he takes great pains to advise us that even while she gives in to these acts of desecration, Mademoiselle Vinteuil retains a virtuous core, which is the source of her discretion, her scruples. She has an "instinctive rectitude," and a "gentility beyond her control."[20] It is not a matter of conscious gestures that have been learned: The archaic self is used to offering recognition and attention to others. Everything proves the "true moral nature" of Mademoiselle Vinteuil, her "goodness of heart," her "naturally virtuous" self.[21] Now we are facing the second protagonist of the conflict: the timid maiden with a "sensitive heart."[22]

This new juncture between personal and communal elements,

ending in the formation of an archaic self, is something that specifically characterizes Mademoiselle Vinteuil. She owes it essentially to her childhood; this archaic self is a product of imitation and transmission. In fact, the narrator likes to bring out all the similarities between Mademoiselle Vinteuil and her father. In a scene recounted several pages before (and recalled here), we see the father remove his music from the piano so that he will not be suspected of immodesty, and, at the same time, he calls attention to this action in exactly the same way that his daughter moves his portrait and has her friend notice the apparently fortuitous removal. Through the scene between the two friends, we are able to perceive, as through a transparency, another interaction, between the father and the daughter; the former scene influences the present one. Mademoiselle Vinteuil is just as careful, even obsequious, as her father; she has retained his gestures of kindness, his mentality. "At the moment when she wished to be thought the very antithesis of her father, what she at once suggested to me were the mannerisms, in thought and speech, of the poor old piano-teacher."[23] Even physically, what is striking about her is "the likeness between her face and his, his mother's blue eyes which he had handed down to her like a family jewel."[24]

Who comes out victorious in the confrontation that takes place over the person of Mademoiselle Vinteuil? After spitting on the portrait, the young woman closes the shutters and the narrator sees nothing more, but he knows that, this time, desire will win out. However, he is not sure that the "trooper" will win out over the "maiden." The narrator rather thinks the opposite: The self of facade imposes itself for "a moment"; the rest of the time it falls back before the maiden, who has many resources, and the enveloping self of Mademoiselle Vinteuil, the internal space in which all these conflicts take place, must realize that pleasure is not in the offing. In vain, Mademoiselle Vinteuil adopts the language of the vicious girl, "the words which she imagined such a young woman might have uttered with sincerity sounded false on her own lips."[25] The all-encompassing self is not the dupe of the self-facade. At the very moment when this self blasphemes the memory of her father, another psychic instance rises inside Mademoiselle Vinteuil and takes its revenge, since the composer's daughter denies herself any selfish pleasure. The "illusion of having escaped beyond the control of their own gentle and scrupulous natures" is "momentary" with such people; "how impossible it was for her to effect it."[26] The narrator returns to this point much later: "This idea that it was merely a pretence of wickedness spoiled her pleasure."[27] There is then, in Mademoiselle Vinteuil, a master of internalized recognition who refuses to give approval. We can glimpse the causes: The internalized object of desire is, with her, torn by contradiction; she wants it but knows at the same time that it is bad. The strategies of the self-facade are therefore quickly thwarted. Proust presents the scene at Montjouvain as a perfect example of sadism, worthy of boulevard theater: It is only there that one "expects to see a girl encouraging a friend to spit upon the portrait of a father who has lived and died for her alone."[28] Reflecting later, however, he realizes that this sadism is not altogether authentic and, therefore, does not deserve disapproval, in any case not as much as ordinary (and much more widespread) spitefulness, which is shown in our indifference to suffering that we have caused. It is the feigned wickedness and cruelty of Mademoiselle Vinteuil that brings this judgment on her. As we have seen, she does not find immediate pleasure in doing evil. She is instead an "artist of evil," since a distance separates her being from her act, which then is assimilated into a work. And in committing the evil action intentionally, she testifies to the fact that the idea of good is not absent from her soul. One must have a sense of the sacred to commit a sacrilege; one must believe in the religion in order to desecrate it. "Her adoration of her father was the very condition of his daughter's sacrilege."[29] For this reason, the narrator finally comes to believe that if Vinteuil had been able to see the scene, he would have found with good reasons a confirmation of the "his daughter's goodness of heart."[30]

One hesitates to follow Proust in this reorientation of morality and justice, which puts all the weight of the judgment on what is known of the motivations of the agent and of her interior experience rather than on the act itself. We have the impression that the vulgarity of a person bothered Proust far more than the violence for which he could be responsible. It is undeniable, however, that regardless of the scene of human interaction, many instances of self are active, and Proust knew how to observe and present a good number of them, causing us to discover the infinite complexity of the commerce between men.

THE MINIMAL TEAM

Let us now try to take up a little more systematically the results of this analysis.

The membrane that separates the self from others, the inside from the outside, is not airtight. Others are not only around us from the beginning, but also from the youngest age we internalize them and their images begin to be part of us. In this sense, the poet is absolutely right: *I* is another. The internal plurality of each being is the correlative of the plurality of people who surround him, the multiplicity of roles that each one of them assumes; this characteristic is distinctive of the human species. At the same time, as soon as they are born, these images—which, of course, are not in any way faithful reproductions of those around us—will be projected outside onto their prototypes or onto other people, subsequently determining our perception of the outside world. The self is the product of others that it, in its turn, produces. This statement does not mean that the human subject will never have access to what philosophers call autonomy. The law and morality are right to want to fix limits to each subject in order to be able to establish responsibilities, but psychology itself mixes and confuses them.

The idea that others around us are responsible for our internal plurality becomes part of classic psychoanalysis through the notion of "censure" (in dreams, for example): a character, often unconscious, who is a result of parental demands and prohibitions and who judges and combats another part of the person. The autonomy of this character was reinforced when, in 1923, Freud gave it the name of "superego": it became one of the three partners of our interior life, precisely the one who originates in the interaction with the others. It is with Melanie Klein, however, that the relation between external "objects" and internal instances becomes the center of attention for specialists. "The inner world consists of objects," she writes, "internalized in various aspects and emotional situations."[31] The terms "introjection" and "projection" are now used to designate this incessant coming-and-going between exterior and interior. Melanie Klein deserves credit for observing that initially the internalized "object" can only be partial: not the entire person but a part of his body. This observation fits well with what one knows today about the mental development of the child: Between the age of two months, when the first internalizations occur, and that of nine months, when the reinforcement of memory allows the firm establishment of the identity of others, the child can actually internalize the parts of the body of another (the breast, the eyes, the hand) as he can his own, without reuniting them in one individual. The transition of the part to the whole takes place only progressively, and the discovery of his image in the mirror can contribute to it.

The metaphor that comes most quickly to mind when we speak of the internal plurality of a person is that of the theater: Our being is like a stage where, as La Rochefoucauld told us, the human comedy is played out. But how can we identify the characters? Even if the parents are, by all evidence, their initial, habitual sources, I hesitate to follow here the far too constraining use Melanie Klein makes, even with the adult, of calling "mother" and "father" these characters that are internalized. In following the Proustian analysis, I would suggest that our internal theater is always animated by at least three characters, which I will call the self, the master of recognition, and the object of desire. Why these three and not others? The only response that I can give for the moment is that this hypothesis possesses a certain intersubjective truth and allows us to take into account innumerable individual situations and stories. We must add immediately that each of these roles can be cut into two, the good and the bad, the positive and the negative, as Melanie Klein has already observed. In truth, the identification of these two poles comes largely from their convenience: All the intermediary positions, all the combinations are equally possible. The duality of good and bad does not need to be reified in the human psyche (it is not necessary to follow here the Manichaeism of Klein, which posits a duality from the beginning: love and hate, a life instinct and a death instinct); it is simply the category that seems proper to designate the value of these internal instances for us.

On the other hand, each one of them can be described in a double perspective, according to how the question is asked: Where does the duality come from? or: What is its use? Let us begin with the role of the self. What is it made up of? It is the result of our perceptions: that of ourselves, of our body, and of our actions, but especially the perception we have of the image others have of us. Lacan is therefore right to contend that "the subject identifies himself, in his feeling of Self, with the image of the other,"[32] even if we hesitate to follow him when he systematically interprets this image as an alienation: In truth, there is no necessary split between the subject of desire and the I of the gaze, for the good reason that without others the subject does not exist, no more than an original "isolation" or "dereliction" exists. Human desire is impossible without the gaze, in the generic sense of the term given here.

The image of self forms and reforms throughout our existence, but its ingredients are not always of equal value; it is suitable here to distinguish, as Proust would suggest to us, between an archaic self and a reflected self. The two are not opposite like the past and present, but rather, on the one hand, more like a past severed from the present moment, a past on which we have no hold, a pluper-fect, as grammarians would say ("perfect," in the sense of "fin-ished"), and, on the other hand, a time that remains in continuity with the present moment, able to situate itself either in the past (but this time a past "imperfect," unfinished) or even in the imme-diate future, when I anticipate the reactions coming from others. The reflected self proceeds sometimes by retrospection, some-times by anticipation, but it always concerns the image that we ourselves make of the image that others have of us.

If there is one unquestioned fact of Freudian thought, it is the archaic self: Before Freud, only a few perspicacious writers realized to what a degree the present behavior of the adult is determined by his past experience, that of his earliest childhood. After Freud, even those who no longer felt at home with psychoanalysis (but preferred a "depth psychology") accepted this revelation. And for what concerns us: At the moment of the present interaction, the individual acts in accordance with an image that he has of himself in the original interaction, such as it was established at the dawn of his life. For there is a period of life during which the self is mallea-ble; it begins at birth, with the first encounter with another, and continues, with a growing intensity at first, then decreasing, until a time difficult to fix with precision: the entrance into adulthood. The self molds itself on the offers and the demands of the beings surrounding him. But once it is formed, this archaic self will harden, and it will have a great deal of trouble in changing again.

It is unnecessary to recall the well-known great ideas of psycho-analysis concerning the archaic self, but we can place them in our perspective. What place should we reserve for the oedipal config-uration? It is clear that the feelings of attraction for the parent of the opposite sex can be duplicated by those of imitation and emu-lation towards the parent of the same sex, just as the rivalry with the same sex can alternate with a feeling of estrangement toward the different one. Orthodox psychoanalysis tries to take this fact into consideration by speaking of positive and negative forms of the same "complex," to which all kinds of intermediary forms can be added; then, however, it is difficult to see its connection with the Greek myth. We come back to the general idea that the relationship of the child with his parents plays an essential role for him. On the other hand, to see in the relationship with the parents only an instance of conflict between desires and law unduly dilutes the specific role played by the family configuration. Furthermore, the place of the child among his siblings, the complicity and rivalry with brothers and sisters are no less formative than the relationship with the parents. Finally, other individuals (nurses, teachers, friends, and enemies) can very soon interfere in this exchange. The archaic self is, therefore, another ministage, on which the protagonists of our childhood play, each one of them able to subdivide in turn.

To recognize the important role of the archaic self in the behavior of an adult does not mean that it is an exclusive determining factor. There is no reason to choose between the "orthodox" psychoanalysts, who believe everything is decided in infancy, and the "revisionist" psychoanalysts, who think the social context is always more important. Both are right: In part, our conduct is the result of multiple factors, past and present, but also, it must be added, it illustrates the exercise of our liberty and, for this reason, remains partly a mystery.

In contrast to the archaic self, the reflected self is not an intangible fact: It changes with time, and we can act upon it, since this image of the image that others have of us carries on a dialogue in the conscience of the self with the image that we have of ourselves, and this dialogue can go from perfect agreement to pure and simple contradiction. In the first case, my image of myself is entirely subject to the one I receive, reflected, from others who surround me; in the second, I object vigorously to this image, in assuring the others that they are mistaken. To those who tell him: "You are well fixed now," the character-victim retorts with anger: "You are all wrong, I've never felt so badly, and don't think you don't have anything to do with it: you are the main reason for my unhappiness."

Mikhail Bakhtin, in his research on intertextuality, has been especially sensitive to the difference between retrospection and anticipation. When Anton Reiser, to take a literary example other than that of *Remembrance*, makes a shameful gesture in front of his superior, there are two reasons for it: It is both *because* he thinks that his superior has a lowly opinion of him and also *to give* him one. Much more often, it is to try to live up to the supposed expectations of others that we modify our behavior in such or such a fashion. At still other times, we anticipate the objections and immediately adopt an argumentative tone. I play the scene in my head before presenting it to the gaze of the other, and at the moment of the presentation, I take into account the imagined reactions of this same other. The reflected self of anticipation is, compared with the retrospective self, more circumstantial and more limited: It depends on the concrete identity of my present interlocutor, instead of a vague average of all my past interlocutors. No more than the preceding one can it be measured in terms of truth: it is a fact, not the description of a fact, and it is as such that it changes my present behavior, not because it guesses exactly the real reactions of the interlocutor.

These are the intersubjective sources of our self; let us turn now to the roles it can assume on the stage of the internal theater. It would be fitting here to point out three: the positive self, the negative self, and the ideal self. The latter is the image of our heroes that we fashion for ourselves; we would like to resemble them, but we clearly see the difference between the ideal and the real. As for the opposition between the good and the bad self, it is rooted in our relationships with others. The demand for recognition that we ask of them is uninterrupted; it is then also necessarily frustrated. Nevertheless, its episodes are lived in very different fashion according to the individual, and each individual can easily distinguish between those dominated by a positive self, who know how to "make the best out of life," and those in which the negative self is foremost, convinced of their own mediocrity or wickedness.

This scenario already applies in infancy: The child can feel himself entirely fulfilled or deceived, according to whether or not he has succeeded in negotiating the especially crucial moments of his existence, the arrival of other children, the separation from the parents and thus the prolonged privation of at least one of them, the abandonment by one or both. The abstract knowledge of this process, moreover, does not allow the best-intentioned and the most available parents to decide in advance the quantity of attention they should shower on their child: A narrow path separates the frustrations of the neglected child from those of the child who is spoiled, and it is difficult to know which of the two will, in adulthood, do him the most harm. For if the neglected child (or the child who believes himself to be) risks lacking self-confidence and so takes refuge in the role of victim, the spoiled child, even if he has more assurance in the beginning, will fear never finding the same attention with others and will choose to fight this fear by a shell of arrogance and rejection. He will thus have been made, in his turn, inadequate for communal life. The positive self can do us harm, just as the negative self can.

Anton Reiser believes that all these misfortunes originate in childhood. Why does nothing work for him at present? "The inexcusable behaviour of his parents in repressing him as a child had so completely crippled his nature that he had never yet recovered his spirit."[33] We note in passing that this blaming of the parents is used here as a remedy (a palliative). Nevertheless, the archaic self constantly intervenes with Anton. But the results of these interventions are not always predictable. If one replays his childhood when he is an adult, it does not mean that one repeats it; altogether too often, one compensates for what was missing. "As he had had too little life of his own, from childhood up," remarks Moritz at another time, in establishing a one-to-one relationship between the attention of others and the existence of self, "the fortunes of all outside him attracted him the more."[34] The original situations did not allow the deduction of present situations or the reverse: Anton is attracted where others would be revolted.

Anton never finds the strength to contest the image of self he receives from others or that he believes he receives. If this image is positive, all goes well; he will make himself worthy of it. "This sense of being esteemed heightened his self-respect and made him quite a different creature"[35] Unfortunately, most of the time the series of circumstances led in the other direction. We have seen that his parents, who had not loved him well, had given him the first blows; he never got over it. Afterward, he would remain a victim of the same spiral: To act well, he needed self-confidence, but to use this confidence, he must receive the esteem of others (or of a particular other). But how can he obtain this esteem since he is incapable of acting well as long as he has not received it? "A certain self-confidence is necessary, which he lacked from childhood; if you want to be agreeable you must think that you can make yourself agreeable. Reiser's self-confidence needed to be elicited by kindness before he could venture to make himself amiable."[36]

Deprived of the initial assurance that love, respect, the attention of parents give, Anton cannot draw from his archaic self the elements of his self-confidence. Could he find them in his reflected self? To do so would be desirable, for "self-respect, which at that time could only be based with him on the respect of others, is the foundation of virtue."[37] In him, good actions are the effect, not the cause, of the good image. Inversely, if the world misjudges him, he loses all interest in himself: "It was natural that as he had no one in the world to please, he paid no attention to his body."[38] As soon as he thinks that others have a bad opinion of him, Anton hurries to confirm it; he is prey to a powerful negative self, to a veritable antiself that destroys him entirely. "The Director's behaviour to Reiser was the effect of his shy suspicious manner, which seemed to indicate a servile spirit; but the Director never reflected that this shy suspicious manner was itself a consequence of his first treatment of Reiser."[39] In this way, the words that others spoke to him took on a magic force: They created what they confirmed, giving the impression of being true when they were just useful. Once again, these opinions are "persuasive definitions," and once more we see the continuity between interpersonal and intrapersonal. La Rochefoucauld had observed the same relationship but in the reverse sense: "The confidence a man has in himself will engender the greater part of that which he inspires in others."[40] If, inversely, the others do not have confidence in me, I have no confidence in myself and so I will not have confidence in them!

In his autobiographical story, *Promise at Dawn*, Romain Gary also has carefully pointed out the effect of the archaic self on the present actions of the person. He knows that "the frustrations felt in childhood leave a profound and indelible mark that can never be compensated for,"[41] but his story is more concerned with the disadvantages of the opposite situation, that of an archaic self that is too positive. When one has received so much in childhood, all the rest of life can seem like a disappointment. "It is wrong to have been loved so much so young, so early. At the dawn of life, you thus acquire a bad habit, the worst habit there is, the habit of being loved. You can't get rid of it. You believe that you have it in you, that you have it in you to be loved, that it is your due, that it will always be there around you, that it can be found again. . . . In your mother's love, life makes you a promise at the dawn of life that it will never keep."[42] There are, it is true, "aggravating circumstances": Gary is an only child, and he not only has no father but his mother has no lover. Now, "they should have someone else to love as well. If my mother had had a husband or a lover I would not have spent my days dying of thirst beside so many fountains."[43]

Romain Gary will spend his life never ceasing to feel the "look of wonderment"[44] of his mother on his face, and he surely owes to this special part of his archaic self his strength and his weakness. He will miraculously escape the dangers of war, will accumulate literary and social honors, will love all the women he wants in a wild forward flight. But he will also become more and more anguished: The emptiness left by the disappearance of the maternal gaze is so vast that nothing can fill it; all reality pales before such an ideal. "A deep frustration, a strange feeling of manhood drained away, almost of infirmity, took hold of me; as I grew older, this feeling grew with me, until it became a craving, a thirst that neither art nor a woman could quench."[45] It is not certain that this interpretation suffices to explain the moods of Gary himself (he wrote these lines in 1960 and committed suicide in 1980), but what he describes here certainly applies to a great number of people.

On the stage of the internal theater, the self (*the* selves) runs into other characters, coming no longer from a supposition of what others think of us but from the direct image that we make for ourselves of others; each character, however, can come from multiple prototypes. Let us pass rapidly over their sources, since these sources are the same: the pluperfect of infant days, the imperfect and the immediate future of social exchanges. But as for the master of recognition, this internal judge who sanctions our acts either positively or negatively (the one Adam Smith called "the impartial and well-informed spectator"), we must be more precise: In childhood, we absorb not only parental injunctions and examples but also social norms, unique to the community. They were internalized during earlier exchanges, and the protagonists are not necessarily identifiable individuals. It is actually a consensus on the ought-to-be without a particular author, made up of customs, of obvious facts, of scientific discoveries, of laws, of proverbs, of clichés, which we record somewhere in the back of our memory without yet knowing what use we will make of them.

These norms concern me not so much as an individual but as a member of a group. Furthermore, they are not exclusively moral; they can just as well be aesthetic. For example, young girls think they must stay thin and eat as little as possible (all the social stereotypes are made use of). Cases also exist, however, in which the totality of internalized values is linked to a particular experience and even takes on the characteristics of a person: a professor, a parent, a close relation, or the opposite, a stranger met by accident; my norms may not coincide with those of the group. For Romain Gary, it was especially his mother who played for him the role of the one he called the "internal witness"[46] and whom he holds responsible for his moral demands.

As for actions undertaken by the master of recognition, they are either friendly or hostile to us, to the point that we cut this figure in two, separating the gratifier from the persecutor. Melanie Klein called attention to them. "We keep enshrined in ourselves our loved people; we may feel in certain difficult situations that we are guided by them, and may find ourselves wondering whether or not they would approve of our actions."[47] Thanks to these characters, we can understand better certain behaviors described earlier. It is the master of recognition who, in his positive version, explains the recognition of conformity: He allows me to dispense with the explicit approval of others, since I know I am in conformity with communal norms; I am therefore, as one says, at peace with my conscience. It is both a positive and a very personal master of recognition who allows for an understanding of arrogance: I gratify myself, even if it is in opposition to the current norms around me. On the other hand, we know how cruel the "persecutor" (a bad master of recognition) can be, who deprives us of all pleasure in presenting us with demands that are each time more difficult to satisfy; the "persecutor" is often responsible for behaviors that qualify us as masochists. He is a pitiless enemy who makes fun of all that we undertake and poisons all our pleasures. He is also the one who, as we have seen, makes enjoyment impossible for Mademoiselle Vinteuil.

Finally, the third principal character is the internalized object of desire (remember, "existence" as well as "living" takes part in intersubjectivity). Its identification does not imply that we must postulate, as correlation, a subject of desire (or *I*), forever cut off from the social self, as Lacan suggests: There is no solution of continuity between the two, which is why the "imaginary" is not a pure delusion or alienation. This image is fed, as the preceding ones were, by our earlier experiences, archaic or recent, personal or shared with other members of our community. And it has the same division between good and bad objects. The good internal object, the assurance of its beneficial effect on us facilitates both the happy love relationship and a certain self-autonomy, responsible for the beneficial influence of the individual. Everyone profits from such an attitude, seen as generous. The bad internal object, the one Fairbairn calls the "saboteur,"[48] is a necessarily unconscious image, for it is intrinsically contradictory and thus more difficult to describe: We are attracted by a certain "object" but at the same time secretly fear it and reject it (probably the fault of the master of recognition). The bad object of desire makes the fulfillment of desire impossible and is responsible for a strong aggressivity toward others and toward oneself, accompanied by especially acute suffering. The disapproval of the master of recognition is easier to rationalize and, therefore, to control, since it has, after all, a certain connection with a kind of morality. But the impossibility of loving and desiring because the object of the desire is in reality bad, the coincidence between the object to love and the object to destroy, is absurd and is perceived as an impossibility of existing (a difference comparable to that of rejection and denial, previously observed).

When the antagonists (or negative characters) win out over the protagonists (or positive characters), mental illness is not far off. When the negative self joins with a bad master of recognition, the door is open to the mania of persecution and to paranoia: The hate, real or imagined, of others creates hatred of self, whose effects are often devastating. All action becomes impossible for me, devoured as I am by hatred of myself faced with the internalized gaze of the other; my timidity is transformed into impotence and "paralysis of spirit."[49] How can I make myself loved if I do not believe I am lovable, if I am not already loved? How can I succeed if I am sure that I will fail? In this way we can create a veritable prison, which we may never be able to leave since the negative action of the subject is fed by the negative reflection of another, which is fed by the action and so on without end. The "inferiority complex" in the adult is often nothing more that a negative reflected self. The bad object of desire, perceived as an aggression no longer against self but against our internalized characters and because of this even more serious, provokes depression and can lead to the destruction of others or of self (to suicide).

The negative effects of these internalized characters are also felt on a collective level. Certain racial minorities have the greatest difficulty in escaping from this spiral: They are believed to be violent and they become so. Their characteristic poverty causes contempt in others, which destroys self-confidence, which in its turn condemns the members of this minority to sink even further into poverty—or to resort to the palliative of violence. As Shelby Steele has shown in his analysis of the racial problem in the United States, the aggressivity of the interior saboteur, of the antiself of the black minority is largely responsible for the hopeless situation in which they find themselves today.

The complexity of the internal scene of a person does not stop there. Jung stated that beside the internalized images *of* others, which he called imago, the individual also produces an image *for* the others, which Jung called his persona: It is a mask displayed to the public, a self of facade. The persona is in a way the inverse of imagoes: no longer the image I receive but that which I produce, no longer the internalization of others but the externalization of self. They are, however, both hybrid products, "a compromise between individual and society."[50] I choose to present myself as likeable or brusque, clownish or melancholy, and in doing so, I intentionally adopt a role, which I know is not "me" or, in any case, not all of me; it can also be entirely determined by the norms at work (resulting from social conformism). Here we have the well-known attitude of hypocrisy, of lying, of pretending, by which I reap a certain recognition but know that it can have come to the wrong person, what is called speaking or acting for the gallery. But it is also the invention, the creation, the enchantment of everyday life, which is transformed into a spectacle and a work of art. This role I choose for myself to play before others can be influenced by the anticipation of their reaction and aims only at charming others: I try to appear so that—I imagine—others could like and admire me (passage from affectation to pretense is easy). But it can also be entirely independent and aim at producing a particular effect: disturb, intrigue, intimidate. The social context plays an important role here (a repressive society evidently favors the blossoming of hypocrisy).

It is important to take into account that this facade-self is no less inevitable than the others: Human interaction mobilizes just one part of the person; I play a role, if only in choosing certain of my traits above others to put forward. Our professional and public identity is obviously a facade-self. For this reason, we will not follow Jung when he sees only one persona for each individual; to the contrary, we produce a multitude of them, depending on the contexts we enter into: public and private, friendly and amorous, of infant or of parent (since we are often both of these). Still, it is useless to want to "divest the self of the false wrappings of the persona"[51]: We cannot separate our self from our relations with others and the demands that we read in their gaze, no more than the "subject" in the Lacanian sense is truly imaginable without its "I." Rather than a mask, the self of facade is a posture, a facial expression: We must always have one.

Finally, to all these characters who act on the stage we must add a last one, which is the stage itself, the frame in which the interaction takes place. There is, therefore, an all encompassing self—but also, in a way, a control tower, since somewhere someone must make a decision in weighing the for and against, the advantages and disadvantages of each solution. This is what William James calls "this self of all the other selves,"[52] which he describes as an instance of arbitration between conflicting elements: "I am aware of a constant play of furtherances and hindrances in my thinking, of checks and releases, tendencies which run with desire, and tendencies which run the other way."[53] Sometimes one must submit to the demands of the master of recognition, sometimes satisfy those of the desiring self, another time obey, not knowing why, the injunctions of the archaic self, yet another remain a prisoner, against one's will and morality, of the reflected self, even of this intentional construction, which is the self of facade (La Rochefoucauld has perfectly described certain examples of these internal conflicts). The all-encompassing self does not intervene directly in this debate, which is sometimes a battle and sometimes an understanding; it is rather the outcome and is situated on a higher level: It is the instance that, following an impenetrable calculation, has us choose between different options, and that fixes the priorities and distributes the passes.

The team imagined in this way is very minimal; each one of its members, we have seen (except for the all-encompassing self), can each be subdivided. And what does not help matters, each person, already multiple in himself, meets other persons as complex as he is: the *you* includes the same instances as the *I*. Each *you*—how many we encounter every day!—calls for a new tuning of our social contact apparatus, or at least a readaptation. There is an admirably delicate instrument in us, of great complexity, which allows us to orient ourselves "automatically" in view of each particular exchange. Novelists have been conscious of this instrument, says William's brother, Henry James, who is fond of phrases like: "He knew that I could not really help him, and that I knew that he knew that I could not do it," or yet again: "Oh, help me to feel the feelings that, I know, you know that I would like to feel!"[54] Such is the everyday of existence, since we live in a permanent negotiation and since human commerce demands the convocation and the cooperation of diverse instances of self. Instances that, let us emphasize one last time, are all intersubjective, produced by interaction with others; none of them comes from the depths of our individual being. It is not this or that facet of our being that is social; it is the entire human existence.

5 Coexistence and Fulfillment

THE FULFILLMENT OF SELF

The recognition we demand of others takes many forms and is always present. But is it the only way to give birth to a feeling of existence? Take the example of work well done. The evidence is that it brings an increase of recognition: I am well thought of in society because I am a good specialist, my colleagues respect me, I have disciples, and besides I am well paid for it and money allows me to have even more gratifications. Recognition remains even if I modify certain circumstances: I can do the work at home and for myself, far from other eyes; in so doing, however, I am duplicating myself in object-producer and subject-evaluator. In other words, I can proceed by self-sanction, congratulate myself internally for having done my work so well. It is possible, however, to find yet another type of satisfaction: not in the judgment brought by others or by myself but outside of any recognition and even of any coexistence, in the very act that accomplishes the work. Without any duplication, without any mediation, the human being has, by his simple presence in each of his acts, the feeling of his own *fulfillment*, and through it he experiences his existence.

The clue that allows us to distinguish between the fulfillment of self and recognition, including its solitary ("arrogant") forms, is the presence or absence of mediation: The recognition is necessarily mediated by another, whether it be an anonymous, impersonal, or internal other; the fulfillment is immediate, it short circuits the process of recognition and contains its own reward. We draw from it the feeling of being ourselves, of living truthfully, that we are sometimes tempted to call "authentic," but the demand to "be oneself," which Oscar Wilde saw inscribed on the pediment of the temple of modernity, still comes too much from self-sanction, since we compare the present actions to an ideal image of self. The same is true of the "realization of self" discussed by certain psychologists. Fulfillment itself, without any comparison, is pure presence. In this aspect, it is akin to the beautiful as defined by Moritz in one of his writings on aesthetics: "The beautiful is so complete in itself that all the goal of its existence is found within it."[1] This completeness is true of each act leading to fulfillment. But even so, we do not abandon "existence" for "life." Even if it is not determined by relationships with others, fulfillment is even more of a stranger to the animal world than recognition was; it presupposes the social nature of man even if it does not make use of it.

The feeling of fulfillment of self that the execution of certain acts or the adoption of certain attitudes gives us does not merge either with what is commonly called the "blossoming" of the personality in the sense that this term implies opening toward the outside, an overabundance of communication, even a form of gaiety. Fulfillment also stimulates joy, but it does not exclude solitude and silence; its effect is purely internal.

Martin Buber has proposed dividing the world of human actions into two spheres, I-Thou and I-It, according to whether or not we encounter other subjects around us. Coexistence is the sphere of I-Thou; fulfillment is the culminating point of the I-It domain. Inside this last sphere, the two sides, passive and active, must be distinguished. Perhaps the most common form of fulfillment is what we feel in being confronted by beauty (since this experience is also fulfillment); I do not find the source of the joy in myself or in the existence of the creator of this beauty, supposing that it has one; beauty is outside me, impersonal, and yet it fills me with a kind of internal jubilation, which reinforces my feeling of existing. When I am immersed in natural beauty, I have a tendency to identify with my senses: I am fulfilled by the sounds, the views, the tactile sensations, the odors; I am fulfilled in a poignant fusion with the world around me.

The beauty of art calls for a more complex perception, for it demands not only the *senses* but the *sense*: that which art gives to human experience. In this respect, art is like other experiences of an intellectual or spiritual nature. When I read a book I admire by a philosopher or a scientist, a poet or a novelist, I feel myself engaged in a relationship that allows me to fulfill myself by just having contact with a powerful thought or an inexhaustible image: My existence seems to truly expand. I can have the same feeling with a religious experience. This experience is not only a community "palliative" or a reassuring "illusion," as Freud thought, but also a possibility for the *I* to open up a world without limits, natural and supernatural, to put personal experience in communion with the entire universe.

To these contemplative ecstasies must be added relevant actions from the active side in the relationship of man to the world. The fulfillment of work well done comes from this activity, whether this work is physical or mental: The production of a work of art illustrates it as well as that of a gourmet dish or of a sand castle beside the sea. Furthermore, the production of an object is in no way obligatory; I can feel my fulfillment in the simple physical effort, when I give the best of myself. A sports feat, like well-done work, obviously comes from a multiple jurisdiction: It can bring me glory and wealth, or it can be done with the simple goal of proving to myself that I can jump higher than the others, that I am capable of rowing across the ocean; but it can also give me joy in the perfection of the act itself, in the fact of attaining what had remained impossible before. I can also rejoice in my mental exploit, in my capacity to solve mathematical problems, without looking for gratification beyond the act itself: My joy is extranormative and is limited to the present moment.

Scientific and artistic creation can be considered the crowning activity here, since it synthesizes the two aspects, at once an interpretation of the world and the creation of an object that never existed before. That science comes from the domain of I-It is true not only of physical sciences, in which the scientist is the only human subject, but even of the social sciences, in which the object is made up of other subjects. As objects of study, they are excluded from the dialogue, but they can take part in it later, as readers or critics of the scientist. This circumstance is also true of the work of art: The artist is alone at the moment of his creation, even if he communicates with his contemporaries before and after.

All forms of fulfillment have a paradoxical character: The *I* seems forgotten here, but it emerges enriched. When I work for the pleasure of it, I do not think of myself: When I admire something or when I communicate, I withdraw into the background. Each time, however, I reaffirm my existence. But this enlarging of the self does not manage to affirm, in some camouflaged form, the isolation of the individual caught up only accidentally in a social network, as different traditions of individualist psychology would have it. Fulfillment is not the opposite of coexistence, as solitude opposes sociality—recognition can be sought in the solitude of arrogance and fulfillment can be lived in the company of others—but as absence or presence of mediation. The world of I-Thou as well as I-It has both detestable and sublime forms; vanity and alienation in work are as widespread as serene communion and fulfillment. Neither of these two worlds is intrinsically superior to the other, and no one can get along without either. The human being is made up of relationships that he has with his fellows, and at the same time, he is capable of intervening, all alone, in the world; he is double, not one.

THE NARROW PATHS

In the course of one experience, multiple mechanisms are set in motion. We have seen it in the case of love, which simultaneously participates in living and existing, in the physical and mental, in receiving and giving, in recognition and communion. This simultaneous experience is also true of the most ordinary acts. I read a book that I like, cozy at home, listening to music: This experience is happiness! Several forms of recognition take part in this feeling of well-being. I am satisfied with the image that I offer myself: The self-sanction is functioning. If someone enters the room, he can admire or envy me: I enjoy refined pleasures. I read an author of quality; I am flattered at the idea of belonging to the (restricted) club of his admirers. But these pleasures, which are sociologically predictable, are still only the most superficial. Beside them, I feel another, more lasting one: The author I read has managed to formulate in words what I felt but did not know how to say, *my* thought, *my* feeling, *my* sensation; in this, he widens my mental universe, he gives it more meaning and more beauty. I project myself into the characters of the novel, and a second life is added to mine. I feel enriched, stronger, more intelligent. But I can also take pleasure in reading intransitively, without going through any mediation, even that of my own judgment. Giving myself over to this activity gives me an immediate feeling of fulfilling myself and, therefore, of existing. Without mentioning the fact that reading comes from habit and so from repetition, which is also a way of persisting in my being.

The complexity of experiences does not annul the interest in separating their elements; it is the interaction of these multiple mechanisms that alone allows us to take them into account. This very complexity obliges us to set aside from the description of our psychic functions the categories that come to mind most readily when we think about life in common—solitude and sociality, selfishness and altruism.

Life in society is not the result of a choice; we are always already social. As the Russian Bakhtin and the American G. H. Mead noted at almost the same time, we can never see our physical selves completely; this inability is a spoken incarnation of our constitutive incompleteness, of the need we have of others in order to establish our consciousness of self and so also to exist. The choice between an isolated life and life in a group is at a completely different level, a choice that reveals nothing fundamental in our attitude toward the world but rather a tendency toward calm and silence or, the opposite, an agoraphilia. Solitude as a way of life does not imply that we can get along without others or that we are not interested in them. All solitude is preceded by a formative period during which it is the relation to others that has oriented our self, and this relation now influences our present life. In solitude we never stop communicating with our fellowmen; we just choose certain forms of communication to the detriment of others. Occasional or indirect encounters can compensate in intensity for what they lose in frequency or convenience.

Rousseau does not contradict himself when he claims simultaneously that life in society defines the vocation of humankind and that he prefers solitude to the company of other men. Remaining alone, he is no less social, since he thinks, ponders, writes. And he is right to be indignant that others see in his taste for solitary contemplation some kind of misanthropy. ("Only wicked people are alone,"[2] a character from Diderot said meanly.) We can be alone in the middle of a crowd and in a deep communion in apparent isolation. Even though he feels happier when he is alone, Rousseau proclaims therefore: "Our sweetest existence is relative and collective, and our true *self* is not entirely within us. Finally, such is man's constitution in this life that one never is able to enjoy oneself well without the cooperation of another."[3] Baudelaire too goes beyond the opposition in terms: "Multitude, solitude: identical terms, and interchangeable by the active and fertile poet. The man who is unable to people his solitude is equally unable to be alone in a bustling crowd."[4] The "universal communion" is even more accessible to the "solitary stroller" than to those who love crowds, or rather it depends not on circumstances but on an internal disposition.

A better comprehension of human existence is useful not only in itself but also because it influences the goals that society fixes for its development. It is because of certain underlying anthropological conceptions that we say the aim of existence is, on the one hand, the blossoming of the individual, the realization of self and, on the other hand, the progress of society, even if it includes the sacrifice of certain advantages for the individual. These two versions of the human ideal, however, are part of the same conception of man, one that pictures him antagonistic to his social milieu and in which it becomes necessary to choose either the individual or society. We must always return to the fact that there exists no previously constituted self, such as capital transmitted by inheritance, which one could squander by distributing it to others or carefully put away behind the shop so as to profit from it at leisure. The self exists only in and by its relations with others; intensifying the social exchange means intensifying the self. The aim of existence could not be one *or* the other—no more self or no more society—but "in hours of miracle," in the language of Saint-Exupéry, "the quality of human relationships."[5]

Even if scholarly theories no longer claim to have their roots in the hedonist principle of the maximization of pleasure or in the utilitarian idea of the greatest happiness for the greatest number—not because one or the other would be immoral but because they account poorly for the real human experience—these principles and these ideals, in the form of anonymous sayings and self-evident facts, continue to impregnate our social life and to direct the political projects waiting in the wings. If the ultimate aim of political forces in a country is only to attain the maximum consumption and the maximum production, without ever studying the effect these results will have on interpersonal relations, a brutal awakening awaits us. We cannot allow ourselves to hide the essential in this way. To become conscious that the aim of human desire is not pleasure but the relation between men can permit us both to be reconciled to situations that would seem unsatisfactory by other criteria and to act in a way that would make life in society better in a lasting and general fashion.

Human existence is not threatened by isolation, for this condition is impossible; it is threatened by certain forms of communication, impoverishing and alienating, and also by individualist representations of our current existence, which make us live as tragedy that which is the human condition itself—our original incompleteness and the need we have of others. For these representations are not a passive reflection of the real; they determine our values and thereby influence reality. These representations make so many individuals, Don Juan, for instance, see attachments to others as chains or at least as paralyzing nets. Benjamin Constant spent his life fighting this paradox, which does not exist—how to defend the political autonomy of the individual while claiming his extreme social dependence? "Bizarre humankind!" he exclaimed in his *Journal*, "which can never be independent."[6] But dependence is not alienating; sociality is not cursed, it is liberating. We must get rid of the individualistic illusions. There is no fulfillment outside relationships with others. Comfort, recognition, cooperation, imitation, competition, communion with others can be lived with happiness.

The social behavior of man is the terrain on which morality is built, and, therefore, it is important to separate the description of moral choices from the mechanism of the psyche itself. Nothing has harmed the understanding of specifically human existence as much as seeing it in exclusively moral terms, such as "vanity" or "thirst for glory." To morally justify our alleged primordial selfishness does not get us any further. We must not see in sociality either a good quality to develop or a flaw to eradicate, and we must not reduce it to generosity or vanity. Every single person has the right to existence, and to attain it he seeks the gaze of others. This seeking is in no way to be condemned. Not coming from any kind of choice, it is by definition extramoral. To live in society is not to "overcome our inclinations" (the demand Kant made to our moral actions). This condition does not mean that selfishness and altruism do not exist or are equivalent but rather that their distinction in no way influences our sociality. If from the moral point of view, altruistic behavior is preferable, it does not follow—as we have seen in the case of devotion—that it is "unselfish" (selfish-unselfish is another couple of terms whose descriptive value is, in psychology, next to zero) or that it produces an unmixed good. Psychology cannot replace morality, contrary to what is sometimes claimed; only a new morality can substitute for the collapse of the old one. Solidarity and a cooperative attitude is morally preferable to its opposite, and, on the other hand, the autonomy of each individual is a value. But human sociality, we repeat, simply has no opposite.

It would be equally useless to try to put in moral opposition the distinction between coexistence and fulfillment: No more than it could be reduced to that of sociality and solitude, it would be impossible to make it the base for the evil of dispersion and the virtue of autarky or concentration, as it seems so many ancient and modern moralists would like for us to do. The feeling of existence drawn from accomplishment is in no way more virtuous than that which comes from recognition; it is just more peaceful. Existence in itself cannot be measured in terms of good or evil but as happiness and unhappiness.

Does this condition mean that since the attitudes reputed to be moral, such as generosity or devotion, find reward in themselves, we should not consider them more virtuous than their opposite? If so, it would still confuse two distinct perspectives, that of psychology of the individual and that of the common good. From the psychological point of view, selfishness and generosity are not opposed as the presence or absence of benefits for the subject or as a concern for oneself or a concern for others, but rather as the choice of limited immediate material benefits and psychic benefits that are indirect but essential. If I make an instrument of another, if I reduce him to the role of a source of immediate pleasure, I deprive myself of infinitely superior gifts he could offer me. From a political point of view, selfishness is regrettable; altruism or self-sacrifice is desirable.

A psychological analysis of moral acts does not take away from their value and even adds to their attraction. Moreover, it can exercise a certain influence on the formulation of the moral ideal. We have seen that the master of recognition could act like a piti-less tyrant, still more severe than the "discipline" with which the monks had formerly castigated themselves and, by its constantly renewed demands, forever prevent any happiness. Having made this statement, however, must we rush to the other extreme and decide in advance that everything we do is equally good, that we should give up any ideal and any attempt at moral perfection? Once more, here is another sterile alternative, yet another brutal application of the law of the excluded third. Between resigned realism and repressive idealism the path of daily virtues lies open, not too distant from our possibilities, since they consist essentially of concern for another and for the others, of which, at any rate, we have the greatest need. Morality does not oblige us to fight our own nature, contrary to what Christianity, as well as Kant, teaches us. To have concern for others does not in any way mean to de-prive oneself but rather the opposite; to see this fact more clearly can favor the common good as much as the happiness of the individual.

But this same conclusion, which could appear to be in praise of communal life, ought to make us conscious of the threats to it. Rousseau, whom we have seen was the first in the West able to identify the basic sociality of our species, did not fail to notice it. There is no happiness without others, he said. "I do not conceive how someone who needs nothing can love anything. I do not conceive how someone who loves nothing can be happy."[7] We are happy because we love; we love because without the other, we are incomplete. If our happiness depends exclusively on others, however, these others also hold the potential instruments of its destruction. "The disorder of our lives arises from our affections far more than from our needs."[8] Physical and material needs are, after all, easy to satisfy, even if a large part of the world's population does not yet manage to do so; affections constitute the essential part of our lives, and they depend on others. "The more he [man] increases his attachments, the more he multiplies his pains."[9] At first, to increase his attachments means to reinforce his feeling of existing, but in thus making himself dependent on others, he takes enormous risks, for "all that we love will escape us sooner or later, and we hold onto it as if it were going to last eternally."[10]

Such is the specific contradiction of the human condition. Our conscience and our desires live in a perpetual present and move in the infinite; our existence happens inside of time and has only a finite extension. "From where does man's weakness come? From the inequality between his strength and his desires. It is our passions that make us weak, because to satisfy them we would need more strength than nature gives us."[11] There is no happiness outside of love, and love is mortal—that of lovers becomes dulled or diluted, that of parents and children is transformed as the children, in their turn, become adults.

Society itself exists in time, and its equilibrium is necessarily precarious; we must not hope that conflicts will disappear but only that they are settled without violence. As for individuals, they cannot command their own desires, even less those of others, and desires change. However, men dream of absolutes. Two of Romain Gary's characters have this exchange in the dark: "—Aline.—Yes?—What is everyone afraid of?—That it won't last —."[12] Barely caught sight of, the unstable equilibrium of recognition by taking turns is broken; hardly attained, the accomplishment of self demands that we begin our conquest again. A very narrow

Afterword to the English Edition

I would like to take the opportunity offered me by this English-language edition to point out several publications in the same area of study that have appeared since the original edition of 1995.

First of all, let me correct an omission and mention here the work of Axel Honneth, especially *Kampf um Anerkennung* (Suhr-kamp, 1992), translated as *The Struggle for Recognition* (Polity Press, 1995; MIT Press, 1996). Honneth's study is in many ways parallel to the present book as both are primarily concerned with the concept of recognition. Honneth begins as I do, but before I did, by recre-ating the intellectual context from which the idea comes, but his reading of Hegel, especially Hegel's youthful writings, is much more detailed and subtle than mine.

He finds support, as I do, in the empirical work of social psy-chology, on the one hand, and in the psychoanalytic study of "ob-ject relations," on the other. His work also makes reference to multiple traditions (with the exception of literature). Because of this very proximity, I would like to point out several divergences in interpretation that still exist (we have already had an amicable discussion of these differences at the invitation of the University of Louvain in 1998).

The first appears on reading the title of Honneth's work, since recognition here is considered inseparable from combat. This soli-darity of the two concepts is found in the work of all those who begin with the Hegelian tradition (I am also thinking of Jessica Benjamin). In the present book, I wanted to show that if one began with Rousseau instead of Hegel, the two could be dissociated and we could conceive of a recognition that is not the result of combat. Honneth points out the anteriority of Rousseau, "another theory leads back to Rousseau" (1996:185), but he does not give him the same importance that I do.

The second divergence concerns the articulation between the different forms of recognition. Honneth distinguishes especially between *self-confidence, self-respect*, and *self-esteem* (see the summary table, 1996:129). This analysis seems accurate to me, but it does not adequately show the subcategories that produce this variety. On the one hand, dimensions vary as to the entity that is the source of recognition—one or several individuals, the community I belong to, or all of humanity (I am both an individual, a citizen, and a human being). On the other hand, the actual form of recognition varies (as I show in the present book); it is either one of conformity or of distinction. The union of these two criteria allows us to identify a larger number of forms of recognition, as well as seeing on which occasion we may pass from one category to the other.

My book is dedicated to François Flahault, whose conversation often inspired me. He has since published a work touching on these same subjects and entitled *La Méchanceté* (Descartes & Cie, 1998), which could be translated as "wickedness."

To define the origins of wickedness, Flahault finds it necessary to speak of a "general anthropology," just as Honneth does. He finds his inspiration in the philosophical tradition as well as with the psychoanalysts, in writers (Mary Shelley, Godwin, and Milton play especially important roles), and also—something I did not do—in his personal memories. In this short space, I can only recommend the reading of Flahault's book, which throws new light on notions such as self-awareness or the feeling of existence.

My own work since 1995 has been less concerned with the analysis of living together than with the history of thought, and what I have presented in shortened form in the first chapter here can be found in more depth (and resituated) in the framework of a new volume, *Le Jardin imparfait* (Grasset, 1998). This work is devoted to the history of humanist thought in France, and Rousseau is once again one of the principal characters. One of my chapters takes up the "interdependence" (among human beings), another considers "love," and they confirm the subject of the present book.

In closing I would like to point out that the journal *New Literary History* (27, no. 1 [winter 1996]) honored me in 1996 by organizing a debate on a preliminary version of the first chapter of this book. The reactions of the participants published there are followed by my commentary entitled "The Gaze and the Fray." Another development of the present research appeared in 1997 in *Partisan Review* (64, no. 3 [summer 1997]: 375–83) as "The Labor of Love." But the subject is far from exhausted!

Tzvetan Todorov

Notes

Canonical translations have been used in the text and cited in the notes. In some cases a published English translation does not exist, or the translators have found it more expedient to provide their own translation; such cases are indicated with "translation ours" and a citation to the French edition.

I   A BRIEF LOOK AT THE HISTORY OF THOUGHT

1   Montaigne, *Essays*, 177.
2   Montaigne, *Essays*, 182.
3   La Bruyère, *Characters*, 199.
4   Pascal, *Pensées*, 47.
5   La Rochefoucauld, *Maxims*, 47, 48.
6   Pascal, *Pensées*, 43.
7   La Rochefoucauld, *Maxims*, 49.
8   Pascal, *Pensées*, 33.
9   Kant, *Universal History*, 6.
10   Kant, *Anthropology*, 135.
11   Kant, *Anthropology*, 136.
12   La Rochefoucauld, *Maximes*, "Avis au lecteur" (translation ours).
13   Diderot, "Bougainville's 'Voyage'" in *Rameau's Nephew*, 228.
14   Sade, *Philosophy in the Bedroom*, 323.
15   Nietzsche, *Will to Power*, 340.
16   Nietzsche, *Will to Power*, 374.
17   Aristotle, *Eudemian Ethics*, 445.
18   Cicero, *On Old Age and On Friendship*, 81.
19   Aristotle, *Politics*, 4–5.
20   Plato, *The Symposium*, 32.
21   Rousseau, *Discourses*, 125.
22   Rousseau, *Dialogues*, 118.

23 Rousseau, *Dialogues*, 9.

24 Rousseau, *Discourses*, 166.

25 Rousseau, *Discourses*, 166.

26 Rousseau, *Discourses*, 273.

27 Rousseau, *Emile*, 221.

28 Rousseau, *Dialogues*, 116.

29 Rousseau, *Discourses*, 166.

30 Rousseau, *Discourses*, 187.

31 Rousseau, *Dialogues*, 112.

32 Rousseau, *Dialogues*, 112.

33 Smith, *Theory of Moral Sentiments*, 50.

34 Smith, *Theory of Moral Sentiments*, 51

35 Smith, *Theory of Moral Sentiments*, 116.

36 Smith, *Theory of Moral Sentiments*, 61.

37 Smith, *Theory of Moral Sentiments*, 51.

38 Smith, *Theory of Moral Sentiments*, 56.

39 Smith, *Theory of Moral Sentiments*, 56.

40 Smith, *Theory of Moral Sentiments*, 50.

41 Smith, *Theory of Moral Sentiments*, 116.

42 Smith, *Theory of Moral Sentiments*, 65.

43 Dupuy, *Sacrifice et l'Envie*, 86 (translation ours).

44 Dupuy, *Sacrifice et l'Envie*, 86 (translation ours).

45 Dupuy, *Sacrifice et l'Envie*, 102 (translation ours).

46 Smith, *Theory of Moral Sentiments*, 312.

47 Smith, *Theory of Moral Sentiments*, 128–30.

48 Smith, *Theory of Moral Sentiments*, 110.

49 Montaigne, *Essays*, 824.

50 Smith, *Theory of Moral Sentiments*, 130.

51 Smith, *Theory of Moral Sentiments*, 137.

52 Kojève, *Reading of Hegel*, 42.

53 Kojève, *Reading of Hegel*, 7.

54 Kojève, *Reading of Hegel*, 6, 43.

55 Kojève, *Reading of Hegel*, 5.

56 Kojève, *Reading of Hegel*, 40.

57 Rousseau, *Discourses*, 184.

58 Kojève, *Reading of Hegel*, 7.

59 Kojève, *Reading of Hegel*, 40–41.

60 Kojève, *Reading of Hegel*, 6.

61 Kojève, *Reading of Hegel*, 19.

62 Kojève, *Reading of Hegel*, 43.

63 Kojève, *Reading of Hegel*, 43.

64 Kojève, *Reading of Hegel*, 41.

65 Freud, *Civilization*, 111–12.

66 Freud, *Civilization*, 97.

67 Freud, *Civilization*, 112.

68 Kant, *Universal History*, 6.

69 Laplanche and Pontalis, *Language of Psychoanalysis*, 256.

70 Adler, *Understanding Human Nature*, 64.

71 Adler, *Social Interest*, 97.

72 Adler, *Social Interest*, 239.

73 Adler, *Understanding Human Nature*, 161.

74 Adler, *Social Interest*, 214.

75 Adler, *Le Sens de la vie,* (translation of French ours).

76 Adler, *Understanding Human Nature,* 28; *Social Interest*, 283.

77 Adler, *Understanding Human Nature*, 28.

78 Adler, *Social Interest*, 221.

79 Adler, *Understanding Human Nature*, 28, 120.

80 Adler, *Understanding Human Nature*, 194.

81 Adler, *Understanding Human Nature*, 70.

82 Adler, *Understanding Human Nature*, 70.

83 Adler, *Understanding Human Nature*, 40.

84 Adler, *Understanding Human Nature*, 72.

85 Bataille, *Eroticism*, 167–68.

86 Bataille, *Eroticism*, 172.

87 Bataille, *Eroticism*, 180.

88 Bataille, *Eroticism*, 167.

89 Bataille, *Eroticism*, 168.

90 Bataille, *Eroticism*, 193.

91 Bataille, *Eroticism*, 171.

92 Bataille, *Eroticism*, 172.

93 Bataille, *Eroticism*, 180.

94 Bataille, *Eroticism*, 174.

95 Bataille, *Eroticism*, 170.

96 Dupuy, *Le Sacrifice et l'Envie,* 101 (translation ours).

97 Luke 6:35, *New Jerusalem Bible*.

98 Fromm, *Escape from Freedom*, 11–12. See also Fromm, *Sigmund Freud's Mission*, 88–91, and Fromm, *Crisis of Psychoanalysis*, 60–61.

99 Fairbairn, *Objects-Relations Theory*, 82.

2 TO BE, TO LIVE, TO EXIST

1 Kant, *Anthropology*, 143.
2 Freud, *Introductory Lectures on Psychoanalysis*, 107.
3 Laplanche and Pontalis, *Language of Psychoanalysis*, 346.
4 Spinoza, *Ethics*, 91.
5 Fromm, *Heart of Man*, 50.
6 Moritz, *Anton Reiser*, 404.
7 Rousseau, *Reveries*, 68–69.
8 Rousseau, *Reveries*, 69.
9 Schopenhauer, "Wisdom of Life," 42.
10 Moritz, *Anton Reiser*, 145.
11 Moritz, *Anton Reiser*, 149.
12 James, *Principles of Psychology*, 281.
13 Smith, *Theory of Moral Sentiments*, 51.
14 Ellison, *Invisible Man*, 3,4.
15 Rousseau, *Emile*, 221.
16 Sartre, *Being and Nothingness*, 232.
17 Balint, *Primary Love*, 62.
18 Balint, *Primary Love*, 63.
19 Fairbairn, *Objects-Relations Theory*.

3 RECOGNITION AND ITS DESTINIES

1 James, *Principles of Psychology*, 302.
2 La Rochefoucauld, *Maxims*, 58.
3 Smith, *Theory of Moral Sentiments*, 50.
4 Smith, *Theory of Moral Sentiments*, 51.
5 James, *Principles of Psychology*, 295. See also Watzlawick et al., *Pragmatics of Human Communication*.
6 Moritz, *Anton Reiser*, 332.
7 Dostoyevsky, *Notes from Underground*, 33–34.
8 Dostoyevsky, *Notes from Underground*, 40.
9 Edelman and Krall, *Shielding the Flame*, 42.
10 Matt. 6:1–6 *New Jerusalem Bible*.
11 Jones, *Sigmund Freud*, 204.
12 Freud, *Civilization*, 75.
13 Sartre, *The Words*, 112.
14 Mucchielli, *Les Motivations*, 53 (translation ours).
15 Freud, *Civilization*, 77.

16 James, *Principles of Psychology*, 294.

17 Joubert cited in Durry, *La Vieillesse de Chateaubriand*, 1:524 (translation ours).

18 Freud, *Civilization*, 81.

19 Shakespeare, *Richard III*, 753.

20 Sartre, *Being and Nothingness*, 343.

21 Horney, *Neurotic Personality*, 209.

22 Shakespeare, *Richard III*, 791.

23 Moritz, *Anton Reiser*, 139.

24 La Rochefoucauld, *Maxims*, 114.

25 Jung, *Two Essays*, 170.

26 Freud, *Civilization*, 81.

27 Rousseau, *Letters to Malesherbes*, 572.

28 Moritz, *Anton Reiser*, 178.

29 Rousseau, *Emile*, 215.

30 Gary, *King Solomon*, 137.

31 Gide, *If It Die*, 127–28.

32 Gide, *If It Die*, 224.

33 Moritz, *Anton Reiser*, 120–21.

34 Gary, *King Solomon*, 44.

35 Gary, *King Solomon*, 123–24.

36 Gary, *King Solomon*, 11.

37 La Rochefoucauld, *Maxims*, 121.

38 Tsvétaeva, *Correspondence à trois*, 172 (translation ours).

39 Kant, *Anthropology*, 105.

40 Adler, *Understanding Human Nature*, 204.

41 Flahault, *Face à Face*, 110 (translation ours).

4 STRUCTURE OF THE PERSON

1 Montaigne, *Essays*, 243.

2 Melville, *Pierre*, 86.

3 Borges, *Other Inquisitions*, 18.

4 Beckett, *Company*, 7.

5 Beckett, *Company*, 34.

6 Beckett, *Company*, 29.

7 Beckett, *Company*, 31–32.

8 Proust, *Remembrance of Things Past*, 1:175.

9 Proust, *Remembrance of Things Past*, 1:176.

10 Proust, *Remembrance of Things Past*, 1:177.

11 Proust, *Remembrance of Things Past*, 1:178.

12 Proust, *Remembrance of Things Past*, 1:177.

13 Proust, *Remembrance of Things Past*, 1:176.

14 Proust, *Remembrance of Things Past*, 1:176.

15 Proust, *Remembrance of Things Past*, 1:176.

16 Proust, *Remembrance of Things Past*, 1:176, 177–78.

17 Proust, *Remembrance of Things Past*, 1:179, 180.

18 Proust, *Remembrance of Things Past*, 1:179.

19 Proust, *Remembrance of Things Past*, 1:177.

20 Proust, *Remembrance of Things Past*, 1:176.

21 Proust, *Remembrance of Things Past*, 1:178, 179.

22 Proust, *Remembrance of Things Past*, 1:175.

23 Proust, *Remembrance of Things Past*, 1:179.

24 Proust, *Remembrance of Things Past*, 1:179.

25 Proust, *Remembrance of Things Past*, 1:176.

26 Proust, *Remembrance of Things Past*, 1:179.

27 Proust, *Remembrance of Things Past*, 3:264.

28 Proust, *Remembrance of Things Past*, 1:178.

29 Proust, *Remembrance of Things Past*, 3:263.

30 Proust, *Remembrance of Things Past*, 1:178.

31 Klein, "On Identification," 141.

32 Lacan, *Écrits* (Fr. ed.), 181 (translation ours).

33 Moritz, *Anton Reiser*, 331.

34 Moritz, *Anton Reiser*, 373.

35 Moritz, *Anton Reiser*, 286.

36 Moritz, *Anton Reiser*, 121.

37 Moritz, *Anton Reiser*, 208.

38 Moritz, *Anton Reiser*, 179.

39 Moritz, *Anton Reiser*, 172.

40 La Rochefoucauld, *Maxims*, 157.

41 Gary, *La Promesse de l'aube*, 115 (translation ours).

42 Gary, *Promise at Dawn*, 25, 26.

43 Gary, *Promise at Dawn*, 26.

44 Gary, *Promise at Dawn*, 130.

45 Gary, *Promise at Dawn*, 9.

46 Gary, *La Nuit Sera Calme*, 27 (translation ours).

47 Klein, *Writings*, 1:338.

48 Fairbairn, *Object-Relations Theory*, 147.

49 Moritz, *Anton Reiser*, 188.

50 Jung, *Two Essays*, 246.

51 Jung, *Two Essays*, 174.

52 James, *Principles of Psychology*, 285.

53 James, *Principles of Psychology*, 286.

54 Henry James cited in Todorov, *Poétique de la prose, choix*, 88 (translation ours).

5 COEXISTENCE AND FULFILLMENT

1 Moritz, *Schriften,* 69 (translation ours).

2 Diderot, *Fils Naturel*, 62 (translation ours).

3 Rousseau, *Dialogues*, 118.

4 Baudelaire, "Crowds," 20.

5 Saint-Exupéry, *Wartime Writings*, 97.

6 Constant, *Journal, Oeuvres*, 394 (translation ours).

7 Rousseau, *Emile*, 221.

8 Rousseau, *Emile*, 443.

9 Rousseau, *Emile*, 444.

10 Rousseau, *Emile*, 444.

11 Rousseau, *Emile*, 165.

12 Gary, *L'Angoisse du roi Salomon*, 265–66 (translation ours).

Bibliography

✠

Abraham, Karl. *Oeuvres complètes*. Vol. 2. Paris: Payot, 1966.

Adler, Alfred. *The Pattern of Life*. Ed. Walter Béran Wolfe. New York: Cosmopolitan Book Corporation, 1930.

———. *Social Interest: A Challenge to Mankind*. Trans. John Linton and Richard Vaughan. New York: Capricorn Books, 1964. French edition cited: *Le Sens de la vie*. Payot, 1991. German original titled *Der Sinn des Lebens*.

———. *Understanding Human Nature*. Trans. Walter Béran Wolfe. New York: Greenberg, 1927.

Argyle, Michael, and Marc Cook. *Gaze and Mutual Gaze*. Cambridge: Cambridge University Press, 1976.

Aristotle. *Eudemian Ethics*. Trans. H. Rackham. Cambridge: Harvard University Press, 1967.

———. *Nicomachean Ethics*. Trans. David Ross, Rev. J. L. Ackrill, and J. O. Urmson. Oxford: Oxford University Press, 1998.

———. *Politics*. Trans. Benjamin Jowett. Oxford: Clarendon, 1885.

Bachofen, Johann Jakob. *Du règne de la mère au patriarcat*. Lausanne: L'Aire, 1980.

Bakhtin, Mikhail. *Speech Genres and Other Late Essays*. Trans. Vern W. McGee. Ed. Caryl Emerson and Michael Holquist. Austin: University of Texas Press, 1986.

Balint, Michael. *The Basic Fault: Therapeutic Aspects of Regression*. London: Tavistock Publications, 1968.

Balint, Michael, with Alice Balint. *Primary Love and Psycho-Analytic Technique*. London: Hogarth Press, 1952.

Bataille, Georges. *Eroticism: Death and Sensuality*. Trans. Mary Dalwood. San Francisco: City Lights, 1986.

———. *The Accursed Share*. 3 vols. Trans. Robert Hurley. New York: Zone Books, 1988–1991.

Bateson, Gregory. *Steps to an Ecology of Mind*. San Francisco: Chandler, 1972.

Batson, Charles Daniel. *The Altruism Question*. Hillsdale NJ: L. Erlbaum, 1991.

Bibliography

Baudelaire, Charles. "Crowds." In *Paris Spleen, 1869*. Trans. Louise Varèse. New York: New Directions, 1947.

Beckett, Samuel. *Company*. London: J. Calder, 1980.

Benjamin, Jessica. *The Bonds of Love*. New York: Pantheon, 1988.

Blanchot, Maurice. *Lautréamont et Sade*. Paris: Minuit, 1963.

Borges, Jorge Luis. *Other Inquisitions, 1937–1952*. Trans. Ruth L. C. Simms. Austin: University of Texas Press, 1964.

Bowlby, John. *Attachment*. Vol. 1 in *Attachment and Loss*. New York: Basic Books, 1969.

Buber, Martin. *Between Man and Man*. Trans. Ronald Smith. New York: Macmillan, 1965.

——. *I and Thou*. Trans. Walter A. Kaufmann. New York: Scribner, 1970.

——. *On Intersubjectivity and Cultural Creation*. Chicago: University of Chicago Press, 1992.

Burston, Daniel. *The Legacy of Erich Fromm*. Cambridge: Harvard University Press, 1991.

Chodorow, Nancy. *The Reproduction of Mothering*. Berkeley: University of California Press, 1978.

Cicero, Marcus Tullius. *On Old Age and On Friendship*. Trans. Frank O. Copley. Ann Arbor: University of Michigan Press, 1967.

Constant, Benjamin. *Oeuvres*. Paris: Gallimard, 1979.

Diderot, Denis. *Le Fils naturel*. Vol. 10 of *Oeuvres complètes*. Paris: Hermann, 1980.

——. *Rameau's Nephew and Other Works*. Trans. Jacques Bazun and Ralph H. Bowen. Garden City NY: Doubleday, 1956.

Dostoevsky, Fyodor. *Notes from Underground*. Ed. and trans. Michael R. Katz. New York: Norton, 1989.

Dupuy, Jean-Pierre. *Le Sacrifice et l'Envie*. Paris: Calmann-Lévy, 1992.

Durry, Marie-Jeanne. *La Veillesse de Chateaubriand*. Vol. 1. Paris: Le Divan, 1933.

Edelman, Marek, and Hanna Krall. *Shielding the Flame*. New York: Henry Holt, 1977.

Elias, Norbert. *The Loneliness of the Dying*. Trans. Edmund Jephcott. Oxford: Basil Blackwell, 1985.

Ellison, Ralph. *Invisible Man*. New York: Random House, 1952.

Fairbairn, William Ronald Dodds. *An Object-Relations Theory of the Personality*. New York: Basic Books, 1954.

Feuerbach, Ludwig. *Principles of the Philosophy of the Future*. Trans. Manfred H. Vogel. Indianapolis: Bobbs-Merrill, 1966.

Flahault, François. *Face à face: Histoire de visages*. Paris: Plon, 1989.

——. *La Parole intermédiaire*. Paris: Seuil, 1978.

——. "Le renouvellement des idées et la question du sentiment d'exister." *Politiques* 7 (1994): 119–40.

Freud, Anna. *The Ego and the Mechanisms of Defense*. Trans. Cecil Baines. New York: International Universities Press, 1950.

Freud, Sigmund. *Civilization and Its Discontents*. Vol. 21 of *The Standard Edition of the Complete Psychological Works of Sigmund Freud*. Trans. James Strachey. London: Hogarth Press, 1961.

——. *Essais de psychanalyse*. Paris: Payot, 1967.

——. *New Introductory Lectures on Psychoanalysis*. Vol. 22 of *The Standard Edition of the Complete Works of Sigmund Freud*. Trans. James Strachey London: Hogarth Press, 1964.

——. *Totem and Taboo*. Ed. and trans. James Strachey. New York: Norton, 1989.

Fromm, Erich. *The Art of Loving*. Ed. Ruth Nanda Anshen. New York: Harper, 1956.

——. *The Crisis of Psychoanalysis*. New York: Holt, Rinehart, & Winston, 1970.

——. *Escape from Freedom*. New York: Holt, Rinehart, & Winston, 1964.

——. *The Heart of Man*. New York: Harper & Row, 1964.

——. *Sigmund Freud's Mission: An Analysis of His Personality and Influence*. Ed. Ruth Nanda Anshen. New York: Harper, 1959.

Fukuyama, Francis. *The End of History and the Last Man*. New York: Free Press, 1992.

Gary, Romain. *King Solomon*. Trans. Barbara Wright. New York: Harper & Row, 1983. French edition cited: *L'Angoisse du roi Salomon*. Gallimard, 1987.

——. *La nuit sera calme*. Paris: Gallimard, 1976.

——. *Promise at Dawn*. Trans. John Markham Beach. New York: Harper, 1961. French edition cited: *La Promesse de l'aube*. Gallimard, 1973.

Gide, André. *If It Die*. Trans. Dorothy Bussy. London: Secker & Warburg, 1951.

Girard, René. *Deceit, Desire, and the Novel: Self and Other in Literary Structure*. Trans. Yvonne Freccero. Baltimore: Johns Hopkins University Press, 1965.

Grimm, Jacob, and Wilhelm Grimm. *The Complete Fairy Tales of the Brothers Grimm*. Trans. Jack Zipes. New York: Bantam, 1992.

Guntrip, Harry. *Personality Structure and Human Interaction*. New York: International Universities Press, 1961.

Habermas, Jürgen. *Theory of Communicative Action*. 2 vols. Trans. Thomas McCarthy. Boston: Beacon Press, 1984–1987.

Hegel, Georg Wilhelm Friedrich. *Phenomenology of Mind*. Trans. William Wallace. Oxford: Clarendon Press, 1894.

Helvétius, Claude Adrien. *Essays on the Mind and Its Several Faculties*. London: Albion, 1810.

Bibliography

Hinde, Robert Audrey. *Biological Bases of Human Social Behavior*. New York: Mc-Graw Hill, 1974.

Hirschman, Albert O. *The Passions and the Interests: Political Arguments for Capitalism before its Triumph*. Princeton NJ: Princeton University Press, 1977.

Hobbes, Thomas. *Leviathan*. Ed. Richard Tuck. Cambridge: Cambridge University Press, 1991.

Horney, Karen. *The Neurotic Personality of Our Time*. New York: Norton, 1937.

Huston, Nancy. *Tombeau de Romain Gary*. Arles: Actes Sud, 1995.

James, William. *Principles of Psychology*. Vol. 1. Cambridge: Harvard University Press, 1981.

Jones, Ernest. *The Last Phase: 1919–1939*. Vol. 3 of *The Life and Work of Sigmund Freud*. London: Hogarth Press, 1957.

Jung, Carl Gustav. *Two Essays on Analytical Psychology*. Trans. R. F. C. Hull. Princeton NJ: Princeton University Press, 1970.

Kant, Immanuel. *Anthropology from a Pragmatic Point of View*. Trans. Mary J. Gregor. The Hague: Martinus Nijhoff, 1974.

——. *The Idea of a Universal History on a Cosmo-Political Plan*. Trans. Thomas de Quincey. Hanover NH: Sociological Press, 1927.

Klein, Melanie. *Writings*. Vol. 1, 1921–1945. London: Hogarth Press, 1975.

——. *Writings*. Vol. 3, 1946–1963. London: Hogarth Press, 1975.

Kojève, Alexandre. *Introduction to the Reading of Hegel: Lectures on the Phenomenology of Spirit*. Comp. Raymond Queneau. Ed. Allan Bloom. Trans. James H. Nichols Jr. New York: Basic Books, 1969. French edition cited: *Introduction à la lecture de Hegel*. Gallimard, 1979.

La Bruyère, Jean de. *Characters*. Trans. Henri Van Laun. Oxford: Oxford University Press, 1963.

Lacan, Jacques. *Ecrits: A Selection*. Trans. Alan Sheridan. New York: Norton, 1977. French edition cited: *Écrits*. Seuil, 1996.

Laplanche, Jean, and Jean-Bernard Pontalis. *The Language of Psychoanalysis*. Trans. Donald Nicholson-Smith. New York: Norton, 1973.

La Rochefoucauld, François de. *Maxims*. Trans. Constantine FitzGibbon. London: Allan Wingate, 1957. French edition cited: *Maximes*. Garnier, 1972.

Lévinas, Emmanuel. *Totality and Infinity*. Trans. Alphonso Lingis. Pittsburgh: Duquesne University Press, 1969.

Machiavelli, Niccolo. *The Prince*. Trans. Harvey C. Mansfield. Chicago: University of Chicago Press, 1998.

Mahler, Margaret S., Fred Pine, and Anni Bergmann. *The Psychological Birth of the Human Infant: Symbiosis and Individuation*. New York: Basic Books, 1975.

Mead, George Herbert. *Mind, Self, and Society.* Chicago: University of Chicago Press, 1934.

Melville, Herman. *Pierre, or The Ambiguities.* New York: Literary Classics of the United States, 1984.

Mitchell, Stephen A. *Relational Concepts in Psychoanalysis.* Cambridge: Harvard University Press, 1988.

Montaigne, Michel de. *The Complete Essays.* Trans. Donald M. Frame. Stanford CA: Stanford University Press, 1958.

Moritz, Karl Phillip. *Anton Reiser.* Trans. Percy Ewing Matheson. London: Oxford University Press, 1926.

——. *Schriften zur Aesthetik und Poetik.* Tübingen: Niemeyer, 1962.

Mucchielli, Alex. *Les Motivations.* Paris: Presses Universitaires de France, 1992.

Nietzsche, Friedrich. *The Gay Science.* Trans. Walter Kaufmann. New York: Vintage Books, 1974.

——. *The Will to Power.* Trans. Walter Kaufmann and R. J. Hollingdale. New York: Random House, 1967.

Nussbaum, Martha. *Need and Recognition: The Gifford Lectures*, manuscript, 1993.

Pascal, Blaise. *Pensées.* Ed. Louis Lafuma. Trans. John Warrington. London: J. M. Dent, 1960.

Piaget, Jean. *Play, Dreams, and Imitation in Childhood.* Trans. C. Gattegno and F. M. Hodgson. New York: Norton, 1951.

Plato. *The Republic.* Trans. G. M. A. Grube. Indianapolis: Hackett, 1974.

——. *The Symposium.* Trans. Benjamin Jowett. Indianapolis: Bobbs-Merrill, 1977.

Proust, Marcel. *Remembrance of Things Past.* 3 vols. Trans. C. K. Scot Montcrieff and Terence Kilmartin. London: Chatto & Windus, 1981.

Rousseau, Jean-Jacques. *The Confessions and Correspondence, Including the Letters to Malsherbes.* Vol. 5 of *The Collected Writings of Rousseau.* Trans. Christopher Kelly. Hanover NH: University Press of New England, 1995.

——. *Dialogues.* Vol. 1 of *The Collected Writings of Rousseau.* Trans. Judith R. Bush, Christopher Kelly, and Roger D. Masters. Hanover NH: University Press of New England, 1990.

——. *The Discourses and Other Early Political Writings.* Ed. and trans. Victor Gourevitch. Cambridge: Cambridge University Press, 1997.

——. *Emile: or, On Education.* Trans. Allan Bloom. New York: Basic Books, 1979.

——. *Julie, or the New Heloise.* Trans. Philip Stewart and Jean Vache. Hanover NH: University Press of New England, 1997.

——. *Letters to Malesherbes.* In *Works.* Edinburgh: J. Dickson & C. Elliot, 1774.

——. *The Reveries of a Solitary Walker.* Trans. Charles E. Butterworth. New York: New York University Press, 1979.

——. *Selections*. Ed. and trans. Victor Gourevitch. New York: Perennial Library, 1986.

——. *The Social Contract and Other Later Political Writings*. Ed. and trans. Victor Gourevitch. Cambridge: Cambridge University Press, 1997.

Sade, Marquis de. *Justine, Philosophy in the Bedroom, Eugénie de Franval, and Other Writings*. Trans. Richard Seaver and Austryn Wainhouse. New York: Grove, 1966.

Saint-Exupéry, Antoine de. "Letter to a Hostage." In *Wartime Writings, 1939–1944*. Trans. Norah Purcell. San Diego: Harcourt Brace Jovanovich, 1986.

Sartre, Jean-Paul. *Being and Nothingness: An Essay in Phenomenological Ontology*. Trans. Hazel E. Barnes. New York: Citadel Press, 1969.

——. *The Words*. Trans. Bernard Frechtman. New York: Braziller, 1965.

Schaffer, H. Rudolph. *The Child's Entry in the Social World*. London: Academic Press, 1984.

Schopenhauer, Arthur. "The Wisdom of Life." In *Essays of Arthur Schopenhauer*. Trans. T. Bailey Saunders. New York: A. L. Burt Company, 1902.

Shakespeare, William. *The Tragedy of Richard the Third*. In *The Riverside Shakespeare*. Boston: Houghton Mifflin Company, 1997.

Smith, Adam. *The Theory of Moral Sentiments*. Oxford: Clarendon Press, 1976.

Sperber, Manès. *Masks of Loneliness: Alfred Adler in Perspective*. Trans. Krishna Winston. New York: Macmillan, 1974.

Spinoza, Benedictus de. *Ethics*. Trans. Andrew Boyle. London: J. M. Dent, 1910.

Steele, Shelby. *The Content of Our Character*. New York: HarperPerennial, 1991.

Sullivan, Harry Stack. *The Interpersonal Theory of Psychiatry*. New York, Norton, 1953.

Taylor, Charles. *Multiculturalism and "The Politics of Recognition."* Princeton, Princeton University Press, 1992.

Todorov, Tzvetan. *The Poetics of Prose*. Trans. Richard Howard. Ithaca: Cornell University Press, 1977. French edition cited: *Poétique de la prose, choix*. Seuil, 1980 [1971].

——. *Mikhail Bakhtin: The Dialogical Principle*. Trans. Wlad Godzich. Minneapolis: University of Minnesota Press, 1984.

Tsvétaeva, Marina, Rainer Maria Rilke, and Boris Pasternak. *Correspondence: Letters, 1926*. Ed. Yevgeny Pasternak, Yelena Pasternak, and Konstantin M. Azadovsky. Trans. Margaret Wettlin and Walter Arndt. San Diego: Harcourt Brace Jovanovich, 1985. French edition cited: *Correspondence à trois*. Gallimard, 1983.

Voelke, Andre-Jean. *Les Rapports avec autrui dans la philosophie grecque*. Paris: Vrin, 1961.

Bibliography

Watzlawick, Paul, Janet Helmick Beavin, and Don D. Jackson. *Pragmatics of Human Communication: A Study of Interactional Patterns, Pathologies, and Paradoxes.* New York: Norton, 1967.

Wilde, Oscar. *The Artist as Critic.* Chicago: University of Chicago Press, 1982.

Winnicott, Donald Woods. *The Maturational Processes and the Facilitating Environment: Studies in the Theory of Emotional Development.* New York: International Universities Press, 1965.

Index

Index

Elias, Norbert, 59
Ellison, Ralph, 58
Eroticism (Bataille), 33
Essay on the Origin of Languages (Rousseau), 13
Essays on the Mind and Its Several Faculties (Helvetius), 7

Fairbairn, R. D., 39, 41, 55, 60, 74–75, 114, 133
fanaticism, 97
Fechner, Gustav, 49
Ferenczi, Sándor, 38–39
Feuerbach, Ludwig, 38
The Fisherman and His Wife (Grimm Brothers), 91
Flahault, François, 109
Fontane, Theodor, 88
Freud, Anna, 88
Freud, Sigmund, 33, 54, 61, 87, 88, 90, 92, 100, 123; and the archaic self, 125–26; *Beyond the Pleasure Principle*, 48; *Civilization and Its Discontents*, 27; and the concept of human relations, 40–41; doctrine of, 28; and drives of aggression, 51–52; and the internal self, 114; and life drives, 47–49; and palliatives, 96; subtraditions of, 38–40; *Totem and Taboo*, 29
Fromm, Erich, 39–40, 41, 51
Fukuyama, Francis, 85–86
fulfillment, 139–42

Gary, Romain, 102, 130–32; *Promise at Dawn*, 130
gaze, 24, 56, 58; as stage 2, 63, 66
Gide, André, 103
Girard, René, 38
God, 13, 18, 79, 91

Gospels, the, 85
Grass, Günter, 91
Grimm Brothers: *The Fisherman and His Wife*, 91
Guntrip, Harry, 74

Habermas, Jürgen, 38
Harlow, Harry, 61
Hegel, Friedrich, 19, 21, 27, 37, 86; *Phenomenology of Mind*, 19; and recognition, 77, 78
Hegel-Kojève, 36, 68, 94; and the origins of humanity, 22–24; on the process of recognition, 20–26. *See also* Hegel; Kojève
Helvétius, Claude, 27, 32; *Essays on the Mind and Its Several Faculties*, 7
hero worship, 96
Hirschman, Albert, 16
Hobbes, Thomas, 2, 8, 3, 15, 27, 68
honor, 16
Horney, Karen, 39, 93
Hugo, Victor, 58; *William Shakespeare*, 52

If It Die (Gide), 103
internal multiplicity, 113–22
intersubjective psychoanalysis, 39

James, Henry, 136
James, William, 58, 79, 82, 90, 114, 136
Jesus Christ, 37
Joubert, Joseph, 91
Jung, Carl, 96, 114, 134–35

Kant, Immanuel, 5, 6, 8, 16, 28, 29, 47, 147, 48
Klein, Melanie, 39, 74, 123–24, 132
Kojève, Alexandre, 19. *See also* Hegel-Kojève

172